CW01652647

ACHIEVE LEVEL 4

SCIENCE

Practice Questions

By **Gerald Page**

RISING STARS

Rising Stars UK Ltd., 76 Farnaby Road, Bromley, BR1 4BH

www.risingstars-uk.com

Published 2003
New Edition 2003

Editorial: Tanya Solomons
Design: Ken Vail Graphic Design, Cambridge
Layout: Fakenham Photosetting Ltd
Cover Design: Burville-Riley
Illustrations: Burville-Riley; Beehive Illustrations (Theresa Tibbetts); Graham-Cameron Illustration (Tony Maher) and Jim Eldridge

British Library Cataloguing in Publication Data

A CIP record for this book is available from the British Library.

ISBN 1-904591-16-7

Printed by Wyndeham Gait, Grimsby, UK

Contents

How to use this book

Topic questions

(1) A series of questions on all the topics you need to cover for the Science Test, including some questions on Scientific Enquiry. The first few pages cover the harder bits of Level 3 and the rest cover all the content of Level 4.

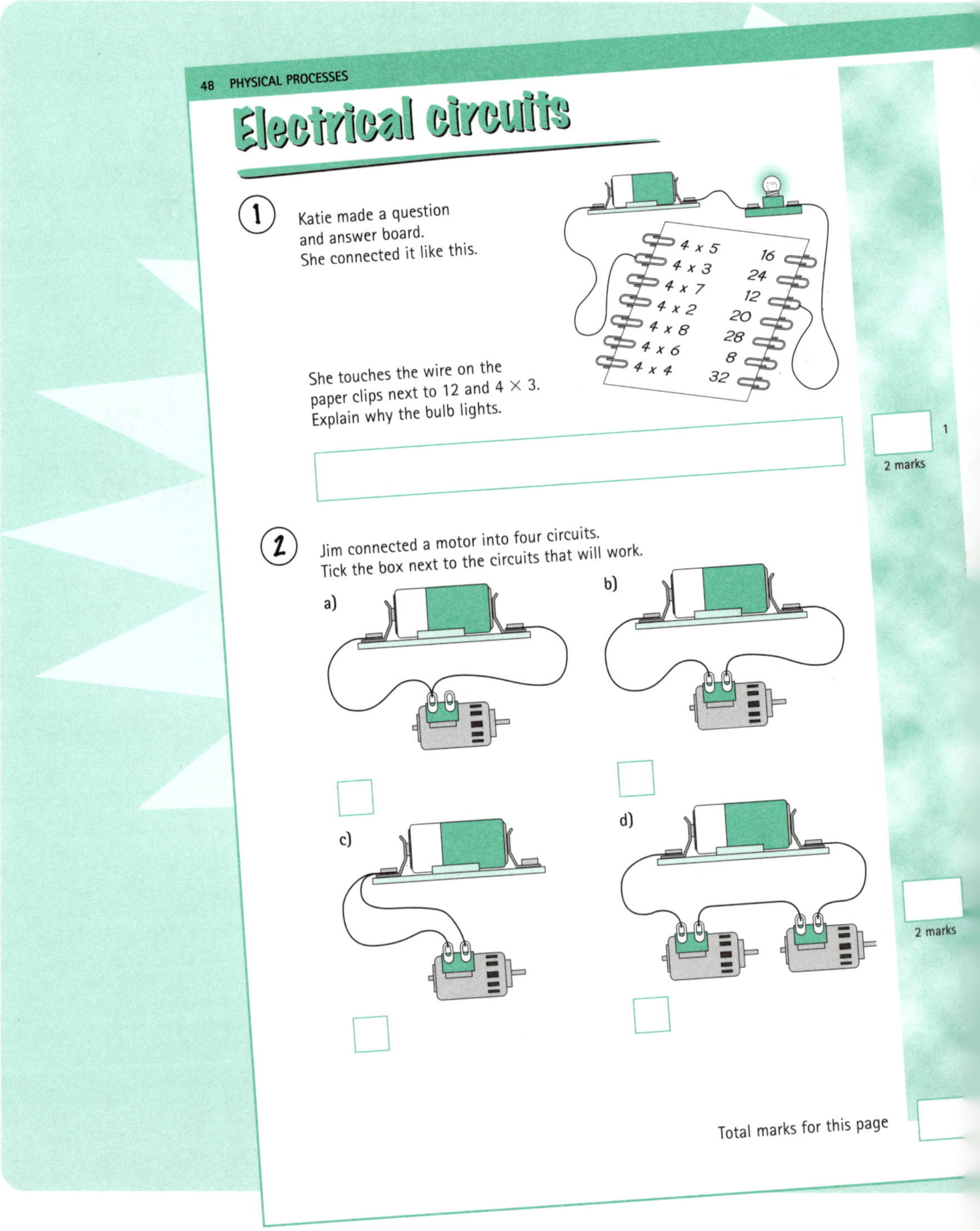

48 PHYSICAL PROCESSES

Electrical circuits

(1) Katie made a question and answer board.
She connected it like this.

She touches the wire on the paper clips next to 12 and 4 × 3.
Explain why the bulb lights.

2 marks

(2) Jim connected a motor into four circuits.
Tick the box next to the circuits that will work.

a) b) c) d)

2 marks

Total marks for this page

2. Each topic matches a section in the Achieve Level 4 Science revision book.

3. Each question has space for the answers, which are included at the back of the book.

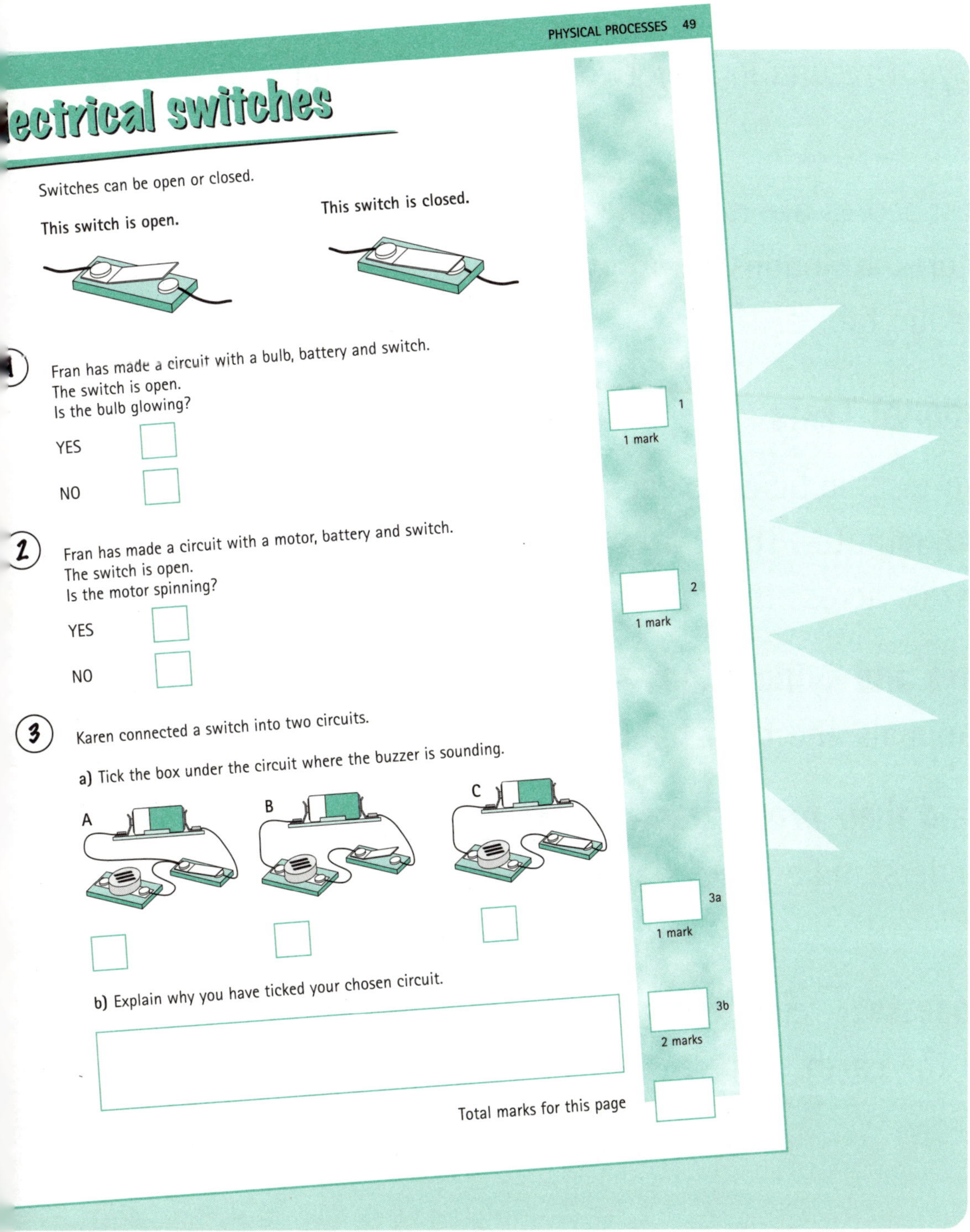

PHYSICAL PROCESSES 49

ectrical switches

Switches can be open or closed.

This switch is open. This switch is closed.

1) Fran has made a circuit with a bulb, battery and switch.
The switch is open.
Is the bulb glowing?

YES ☐

NO ☐

1 — 1 mark

2) Fran has made a circuit with a motor, battery and switch.
The switch is open.
Is the motor spinning?

YES ☐

NO ☐

2 — 1 mark

3) Karen connected a switch into two circuits.

a) Tick the box under the circuit where the buzzer is sounding.

A ☐ B ☐ C ☐

3a — 1 mark

b) Explain why you have ticked your chosen circuit.

3b — 2 marks

Total marks for this page

The 2004 National Tests

Key Facts

- The Key Stage 2 National Tests (or SATs) take place in the middle of May in Year 6. You will be tested on Maths, English and Science.
- The tests take place in your school and will be marked by examiners – not your teacher!
- You will get your results in July, two months after you take the tests.
- Individual test scores are not made public but a school's combined scores are published in what are commonly known as league tables.

The Science National Tests

You will take two tests in Science each one lasting approximatley 45 minutes. These are designed to test your knowledge and skills across the following areas of Science:

- **Life processes and living things** – the human body, plants and animals and their habitats.
- **Materials and their properties** – changing different materials, understanding the characteristics of different materials.
- **Physical processes** – electricity, forces, light and sound, the Sun and the Earth.

Don't forget!

Scientific Enquiry – The National Tests now include more questions that test your *Scientific Enquiry* skills.

The questions will often be based around a picture or a description of an investigation that children have carried out, along with their results. You won't need to carry out the investigation in the test but you might be asked how you would improve it if you were doing the investigation in class.

The 2003 National Tests papers included questions like:

- Write the question that the children were investigating.
- Choose the correct equipment to use in an investigation.
- Complete a table of results from an investigation.
- Draw conclusions from the results of investigations.
- Answer questions about graphs and charts completed in an investigation.
- Describe what the children have found out from an investigation.

You might also have to answer some questions about a famous scientist! In 2003 there was a series of questions about Edward Jenner. He found a cure for smallpox a long time ago and saved millions of lives!

Many of the questions in this book include elements of scientific enquiry but we have also added extra pages with specific questions designed to help you succeed in this new area of testing: pages 10-11 and pages 20-29.

ACHIEVE LEVEL 4

Test tips and technique

Before the test

1. When you revise, try revising a 'little and often' rather than in long sessions.
2. Learn the Key Facts (at the end of the book) so that you can recall them instantly. These are your tools for performing your calculations.
3. Revise with a friend. You can encourage and learn from each other.
4. Get a good night's sleep the night before.
5. Make sure you have breakfast!
6. Be prepared – bring your own pens and pencils and wear a watch to check the time as you go.

During the test

1. As you know by now, READ THE QUESTION THEN READ IT AGAIN.
2. If you get stuck, don't linger on the same question – move on! You can come back to it later.
3. Never leave a multiple choice question. Guess if you really can't work out the answer.
4. Check to see how many marks a question is worth. Have you 'earned' those marks with your answer?
5. Check your answers after each question. Does your answer look correct?

6. Be aware of the time. After 20 minutes, check to see how far you have got.
7. Try to leave a couple of minutes at the end to read through what you have written.
8. Don't leave any questions unanswered. In the two minutes you have left yourself at the end, make an educated guess at the questions you really couldn't do.
9. Remember, as long as you have done your best, nobody can ask for more. Only you will know if that is the case.

Things to remember

1. Don't panic! If you see a difficult question, take your time, re-read it and have a go!
2. Check every question and every page to be sure you don't miss any! Some questions will want two answers.
3. If a question is about measuring, always write in the UNIT of MEASUREMENT (e.g. newtons, l, kg).
4. Don't be afraid to ask a teacher for anything you need, such as tracing paper or another pencil.
5. Write neatly – if you want to change an answer, put a line through it and write beside the answer box.
6. Always double-check your answers.

Good luck!

Finding answers

1 Kate wanted to find out which part of the playground was hottest in the afternoon.
What should she use to measure the temperature?

Thermometer ✓

1 — 1 mark — 1

2 Pat wanted to find out how far children in his class can jump.
What should he use to measure the distance? Tick one box.

ruler ☐ metre rule ☐ long tape measure ☑ strides ☐

✓

1 — 1 mark — 2

3 Pete wanted to find out which type of cloth was best to make patches for jeans.
What should he do to test three different types of cloth?

Pete should take each cloth sample and try them out a few times to make sure the sample he is trying is the best.

✗

0 — 1 mark — 3

4 Terry wanted to find out whether earthworms like damp soil or dry soil.
Write a test that he might do to find out.

Terry should take an earthworm and put it first in the damp soil and then to the dry soil and see which one the earthworm likes.

✓

1 — 1 mark — 4

5 Sally wants to find out which of her batteries is fully charged.
What should she do to test them?

Sally should Put the batteries in something that needs a battery in order to work and then see if it works or not.

✓

1 — 1 mark — 5

Total marks for this page 4

Data patterns

1

Dan made a ramp for his toy car to roll off. He made the ramp steeper by adding blocks. This table shows the distance travelled by the car off the ramp.

Height of ramp (blocks)	Distance travelled by car (cm)
1	10
2	14
3	20
4	26
5	22
6	17

a) How far did the car travel when the ramp was one block high? 10 cm ✓

1 mark 1a — 1

b) How far did it travel when it was four blocks high? 26 cm ✓

1 mark 1b — 1

c) What happened when the ramp was more than four blocks high?

The distance of the car travelled futher. X

1 mark 1c — 0

2

Lyra looked at the plants growing in the open and under a tree.

She thought there was a difference.

She measured the height of dandelions to see if she was right.

Distance from tree (metres)	Height of the dandelions (cm)
0	10
1	15
2	19
3	25
4	25

Explain the pattern of the results.

If the dandelion is closer to the tree the height will be shorter, but if the dandelions are futher away from the tree the height will be longer. ✓

2 marks 2 — 2

Total marks for this page — 4

Living and non-living things

1 Here is a plastic plant and a sunflower plant.
Join up the picture to the correct sentences.

3 (3 marks) 1

It can grow.

It needs sunlight.

It will be OK in a cupboard.

It takes up water.

It will never die.

It has roots.

2 Connect each sentence to either the wooden bird or the real bird.

3 (3 marks) 2

It can move itself.

It eats seeds.

It breathes.

It has no senses.

It will not grow at all.

It can only move if someone moves it.

It cannot eat.

It can see and hear.

It will grow into an adult bird.

It can lay eggs

3 How do you know a living thing is alive?
List some of the things that tell you it is alive.

2 (2 marks) 3

- It moves
- It reproudces
- It feeds

Total marks for this page 8

Plants

1 This bar chart shows the effect of water on plant growth.

- Plant A got 1 spoon of water each day.
- Plant B got 3 spoons of water each day.
- Plant C got 5 spoons of water each day.

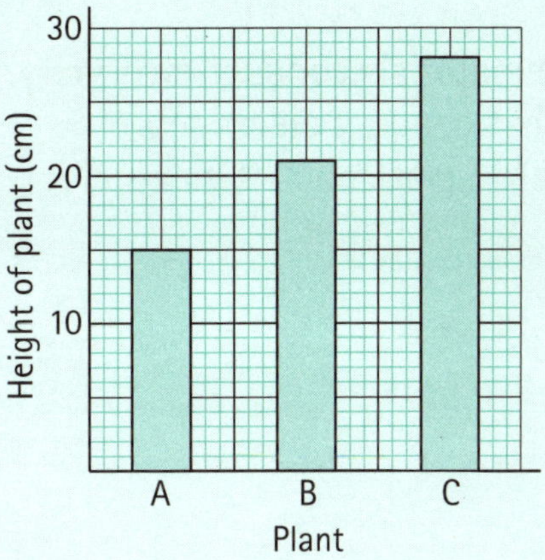

a) Which plant grew tallest? C — 1 mark (1a): 1

b) Which plant was shortest? A — 1 mark (1b): 1

c) Tick the box next to the things that should be kept the same for all the plants in this experiment.

Where they were growing.		The size of the plant pot.	✓
The type of compost.	✓	The amount of water.	✓

1 mark (1c): 0

2 Kim wanted to see what effect light had on the way plants grow. She gave all three plants the same amount of water.

a) Tick the box next to the plant which will grow best. Put a cross in the box next to the plant which will grow worst.

She put one plant on the windowsill.	✓
She put one plant on a table in the middle of the room.	
She put one plant in a cupboard.	X

2 marks (2a): 2

b) In this experiment tick the things that were the same for each plant.

The amount of water.	✓
Where they were growing.	X
The size of the plant pot.	✓
The type of compost.	✓

2 marks (2b): 2

Total marks for this page: 6

Material groups

1 Which of these materials conduct electricity?
Tick the ones that conduct electricity.
Cross those that do not conduct electricity.

- wood ☐
- steel ☐
- plastic ☐
- glass ☐
- aluminium ☐
- lead ☐
- wool ☐

1 — 3 marks

2 Which of these materials is attracted to a magnet?
Connect each to the correct sentence.

copper
steel
plastic
glass
iron
aluminium
lead

is attracted to a magnet

is not attracted to a magnet

2 — 3 marks

3 Which materials float and which sink?
Write the name of the material in the correct set.

wood
wax
steel
glass
polystyrene
lead
aluminium

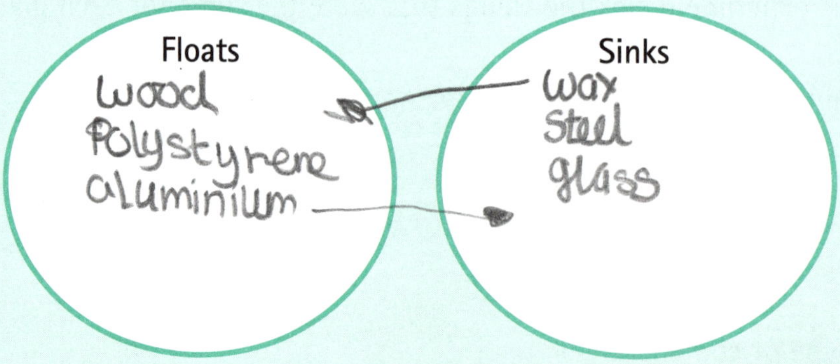

3 — 3 marks

Total marks for this page

The right material

1 Look at this wire.
Label the materials used to make it.

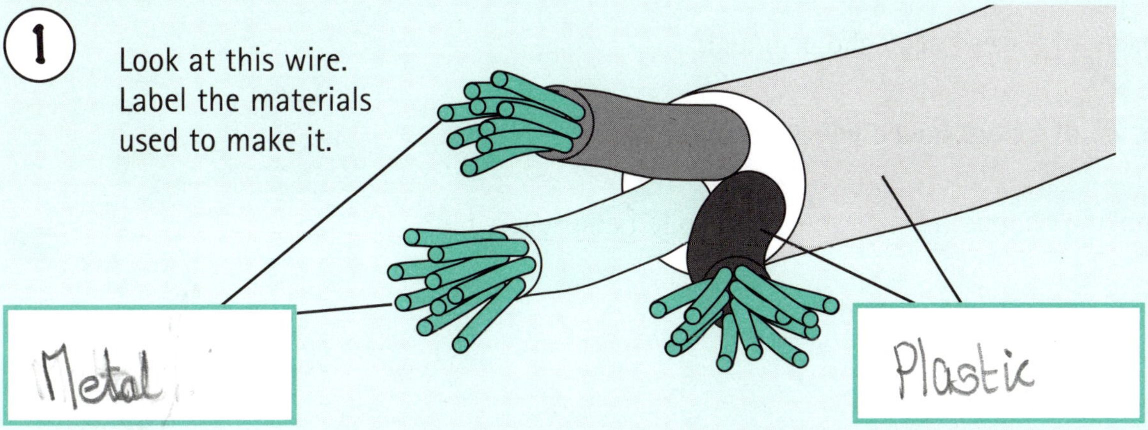

2 — 2 marks — 1

2 a) Why are the pins of a mains electric plug made of metal?

0 — 1 mark — 2a

b) Why is the back of a mains plug made of plastic?

So that when you plug something electrical in, electricty won't conduct plastic so you won't get a shock.

1 — 1 mark — 2b

3 Join the name of the material to what it is like.
Join what it is like to what it is used for on a bike.

Material	What it is like	What it can be used for
glass	soft and feels warm	bike tyres
rubber	very strong	bike lamp
steel	see through	the frame
plastic foam	bouncy and hard wearing	handlebar grips

2 — 3 marks — 3

Total marks for this page 5

Reversible or non-reversible?

1

Is the inside of a fresh egg solid or liquid?	liquid ✓
Is the inside of a hard boiled egg solid or liquid?	soild ✓
Is the cooking change from fresh egg to boiled egg reversible?	No ✓
Is drinking water liquid or solid?	liquid ✓
Is an ice cube solid or liquid?	soild ✓
Is the freezing change from drinking water to ice cube reversible?	Yes ✓

3 — 3 marks 1

2

Write true or false next to each sentence.

Burning a paper is a reversible change because you can use the ashes.	False ✓
Melting an ice cube is a reversible change because you can refreeze it.	True ✓
Evaporation of water is a reversible change because you can condense it.	True ✓
Baking a cake is a reversible change because you can cut it up.	False ✓

3 — 3 marks 2

3

Tina let some fresh bread dry out for a week.
She thinks it is reversible because you can add water to it.
Pete thinks it is not reversible because it cannot be made fresh again.
Who is right?

Pete is right because once the bread is dryed you cannot make it back into fresh bread again.

1 — 1 mark 3

4

Draw a line from the change to the correct sentence.

- freezing water
- burning wood
- baking bread
- melting ice cubes
- burning coal
- dissolving sugar
- making bricks from clay

REVERSIBLE CHANGE

NON-REVERSIBLE CHANGE

3 — 3 marks 4

Total marks for this page 10

Electric circuits

1 Jim has made a circuit.
He unclips one of the wires.
The bulb goes out.
Tick the best explanation.

- [ ] It does not work.
- [x] The circuit is not complete.
- [ ] The bulb broke.
- [ ] The battery is flat.

1 — 1 mark — 1

2 Kate makes a circuit with a bulb and a battery.
The bulb glows.
She leaves it connected for four hours.
When she comes back it no longer works.
Why has the circuit stopped working?

Because the battery may have become flat after all those hours.

1 — 1 mark — 2

3 Explain why these bulbs are not glowing.

a)

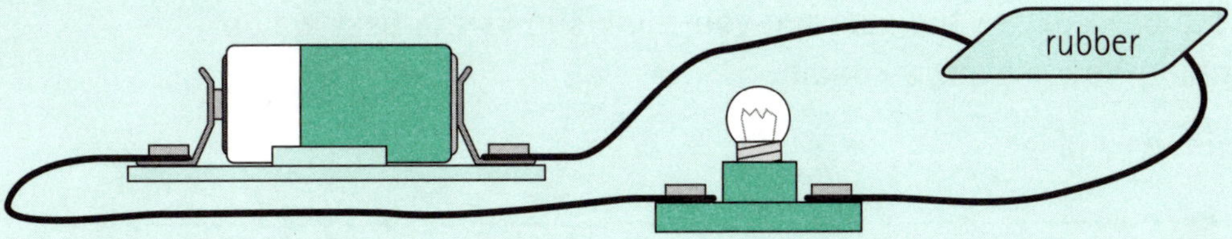

Rubber does not counduct electricty.

1 — 1 mark — 3a

b)

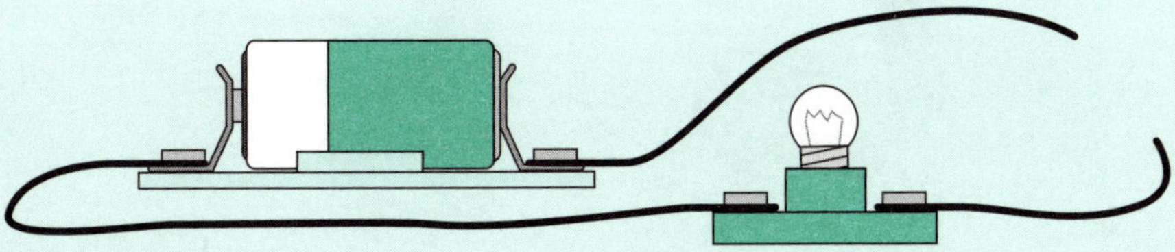

This is not a complete circuit there is a gap.

1 — 1 mark — 3b

Total marks for this page 4

Seeing the light

1 Which of these objects is a source of light? Which is not a source of light? Connect the object to the correct sentence.

TV
Sun
Book
Torch
Flower
Fire
Star

SOURCE OF LIGHT

NOT A SOURCE OF LIGHT

2 | 1
3 marks

2 Here are three drawings which might help explain how we see things.

a) Tick the box next to the diagram you think shows the best way of describing how we see a candle.

0 | 2a
1 mark

b) Explain your idea.

It's always the light source shining towards you not the eye looking at the light source.

1 | 2b
2 marks

Total marks for this page 3

Pushes and pulls

1 Kate is dropping objects into sand.
She looks at how big a mark each object makes.
Tick the three ways she can make bigger marks in the sand.

- Drop bigger objects. ✓
- Drop lighter objects. ☐
- Drop objects from lower down. ☐
- Drop smaller objects. ☐
- Drop objects from higher up. ✓
- Drop heavier objects. ✓

1 | 1 mark | 1

2 Jim is running his toy truck into a wall of wooden blocks.
Suggest ways he can knock down more of the wall with his truck.

Jim could Pull his toy truck more harder.

1 | 1 mark | 2

3 Put these pushes in order from largest to smallest.
Write in 1 next to the biggest push and 3 next to the smallest.

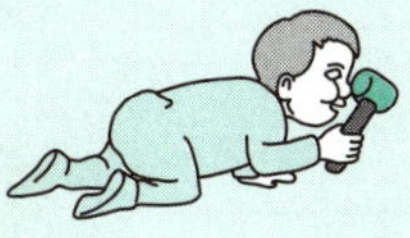
3

1 (2)

2 (1)

0 | 1 mark | 3

4 Put these pulls in order from largest to smallest.
Write in 1 next to the biggest pull and 4 next to the smallest.

1

4

2

3

1 | 1 mark | 4

Total marks for this page 3

Selecting equipment

1 Match the equipment to the units of measurement.
Draw a line from the equipment to the units.
One has been done for you.

ruler	seconds
forcemeter	degrees Celsius
measuring jug	millilitres
beam balance	newtons
stopwatch	kilograms and grams
clock in a room	millimetres
thermometer	minutes and hours

3

3 marks 1

2 Rajiv was measuring how high a ball bounced off different types of flooring.

What measuring equipment should he use?

Ruler

1

1 mark 2

3 Annie was measuring the weight of a rock in air and again in water.

What measuring equipment should she use?

Write the name of one piece of equipment.

Beam balance

1

1 mark 3

4 Garth was investigating how quickly a parachute fell to the floor.

What measuring equipment should he use?

Write the name of one piece of equipment.

Stop Watch

1

1 mark 4

Total marks for this page 6

How can you find out?

1 You have three samples of elastic.
How can you find out which is the stretchiest?
Tick one box.

- Look in a book. ☐
- Look on the internet. ☐
- Do a fair test. ☑
- Just try one or two of them with weights. ☐

1 mark: 1 — 1

2 You are looking at the trees in the school grounds.
How will you find their names?

- By doing a fair test. ☐
- By making a branching key of trees. ☐
- By looking in a tree identification book. ☑

1 mark: 1 — 2

3 You want to see today's pictures from the Hubble Space telescope.
How will you find them?

- By looking in an astronomy book. ☐
- By doing a fair test. ☐
- By looking on the internet. ☑

1 mark: 1 — 3

4 You are doing a project on your class.
You want to find out what is the most common hair colour in the class.
How will you find out?

- By looking in a book about people. ☐
- By doing a fair test. ☐
- By looking on the internet. ☐
- By doing a class survey. ☑

1 mark: 1 — 4

Total marks for this page: 4

Plot the graph

1 Draw a bar chart using this information.

Type of seed	Number of days to sprout
radish	3
lettuce	6
bean	5
sunflower	4

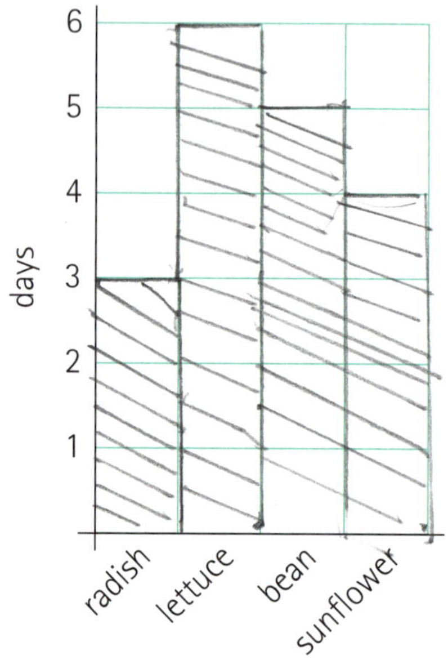

3 — 3 marks 1

2 Label the slices of this pie chart using this information.

Eye colour	Number of people with that eye colour
brown	10
blue	5
green	5

Eye colour in our class

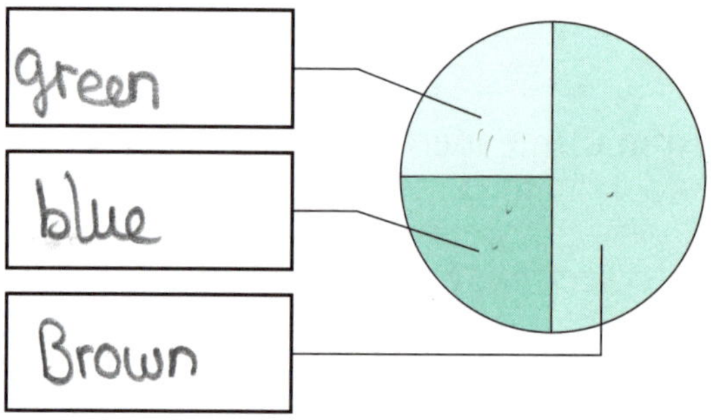

3 — 3 marks 2

3 Mark these points on this graph.
Draw a line to connect the points.
The first two have been done for you.

Week	Height of the sunflower plant (cm)
1	5
2	10
3	20
4	30
5	35
6	40

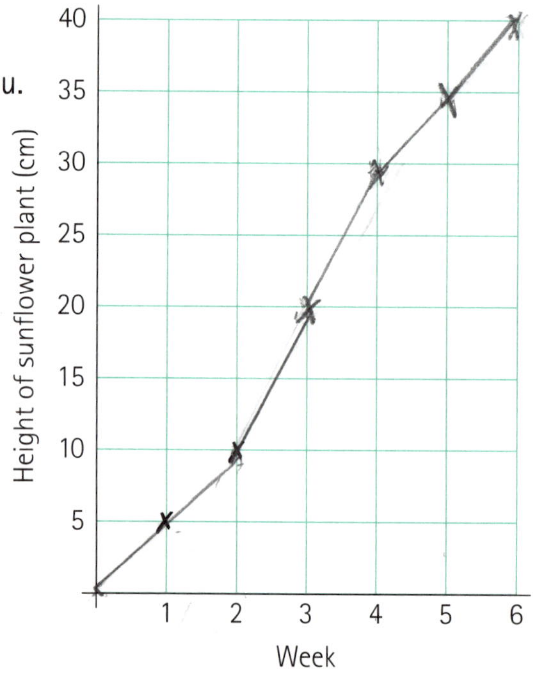

2 — 2 marks 3

Total marks for this page 8

Data patterns

1 This table shows the number of birds that were seen in different places around the school.

In the flower beds	5
On the school field	20
In the area with long grass	9
On the hedge	3
In the car park	8

Where were most birds noticed?

On the school field

Where were fewest birds found?

On the hedge

2

2 marks 1

2 The times when birds were seen in the playground were recorded.

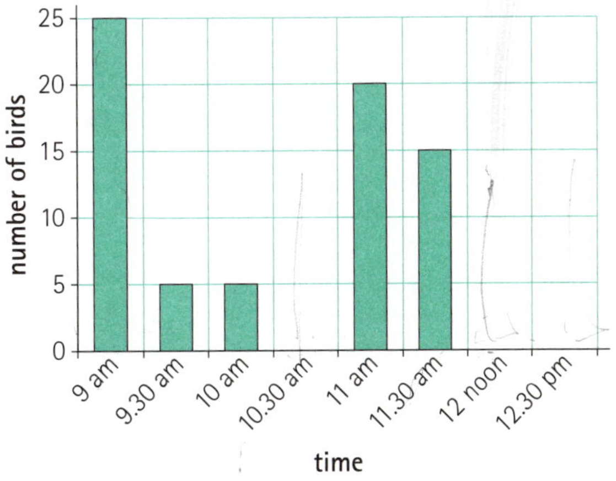

When were there no birds in the playground? 10:30 am and 12:30pm

Why do you think there were none at those times?

Give one reason why there were so many birds in the playground at 11 o'clock?

3 marks 2

3 These pie charts show the type of bird seen in two different places.

Which one type of bird was seen in both places? Sparrow

In which location could more types of bird be seen? Playground

garden

2 1

2 marks 3

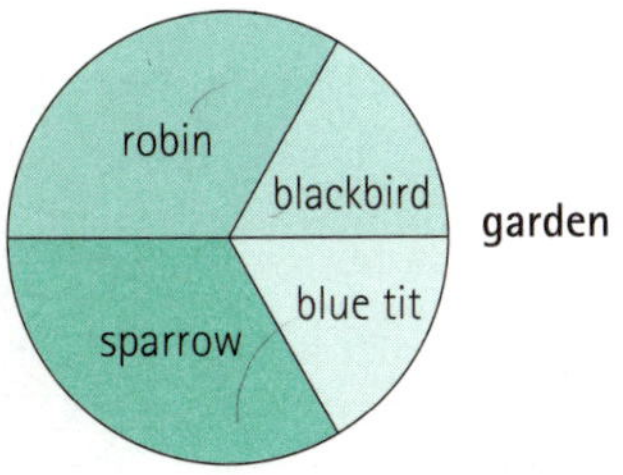

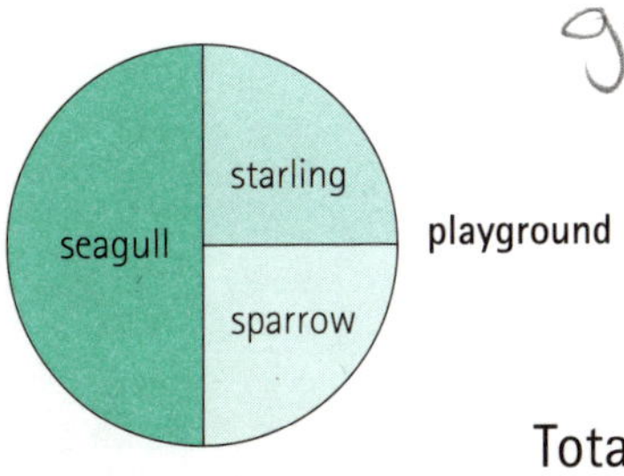

Total marks for this page 3

Changing factors

1 You are going to plan an investigation into melting ice cubes.
You can use different size ice cubes, sheets of material, salt and any other equipment you need.

Here are some ideas to get you thinking.

We can see if wrapping the ice in different material helps.

I think bubble wrap will keep ice frozen for ages.

We can see if putting the ice cubes in different places has an effect.

We can see if putting ice cubes in water at different temperatures changes things.

a) Write here what you would investigate.

I will try to find out

1a

1 mark

b) What factor might you change in your experiment?

1b 2 marks

c) What factor would you observe or measure?

1c 2 marks

d) How would you measure this factor?

1d 2 marks

e) Write two factors that you will keep the same in your investigation.

1e 2 marks

f) Look at this graph. What factor was being changed by the children who drew the chart?

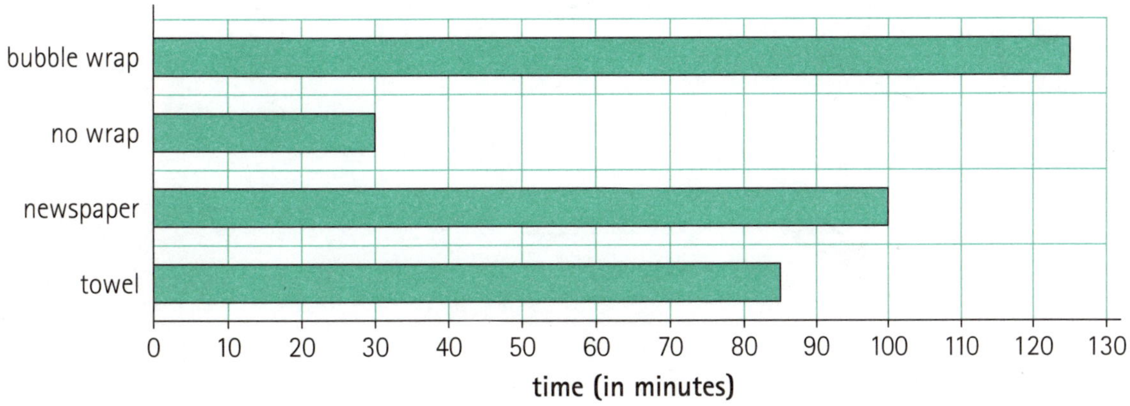

1f 1 mark

Total marks for this page

Predictions

1 Paul is testing the strength of different papers. Paul's teacher asks him to predict which one will be strongest. What factor do you think he should think about?

Tick one box.

The thickness of the paper. ☐

The colour of the paper. ☐

1 mark 1

2 He has to decide which spring balance to get out of the cupboard. Tick one box which shows the best set of masses to test the paper's strength.

weighs up to 1 newton (100 g) ☐

weighs up to 10 newtons (1 kg) ☐

weighs up to 100 newtons (10 kg) ☐

weighs up to 1000 newtons (100 kg) ☐

1 mark 2

3 Paul wants to see if the papers are as strong when wet. What is your prediction?

I think the papers will ______ when they are wet.

1 mark 3

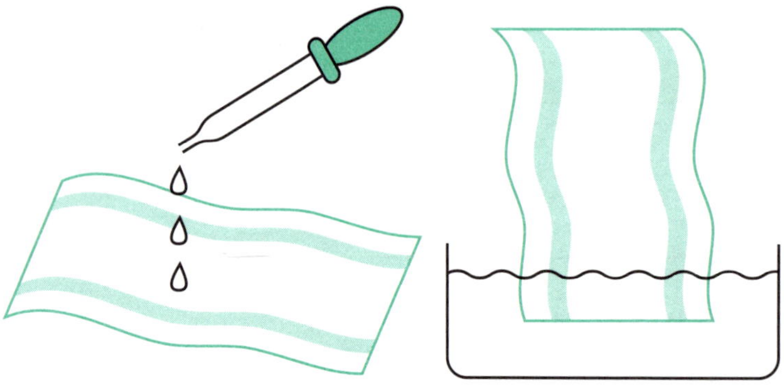

Total marks for this page ☐

Questions

1 Pat is testing different size gyrocopters. She made all the gyrocopters from the same type of paper.

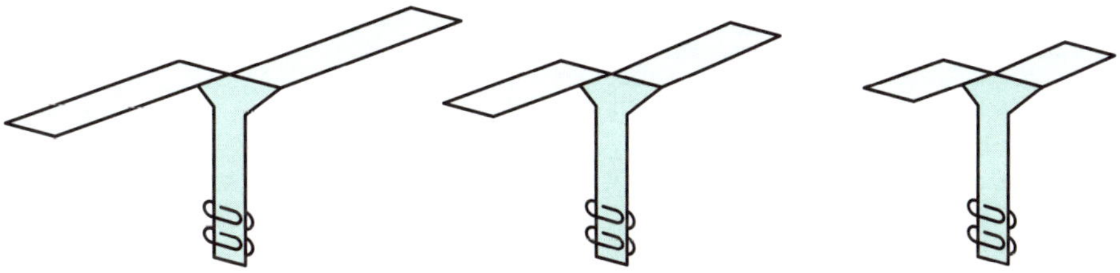

a) Which question was she investigating?

Do heavy gyrocopters fall slower? ☐

Do large gyrocopters fall slower than smaller ones? ☐

Do plastic gyrocopters fall slower than paper ones? ☐

Do heavy gyrocopters fall slower than light ones? ☐

1a ☐ 1 mark

b) This table shows the results of her test.

Length of the wing of the gyrocopter	2 cm	4 cm	6 cm
Time taken to fall	1 second	2 seconds	2.5 seconds

Tick the correct box.

Gyrocopters with longer wings fall slower. ☐

Gyrocopters with shorter wings fall slower. ☐

All gyrocopters fall at the same speed. ☐

1b ☐ 1 mark

2 Plan an investigation into changing the number of paper clips on a gyrocopter.

a) Write the only thing you would change.

☐

2a ☐ 1 mark

b) Write one thing you would keep the same.

☐

2b ☐ 1 mark

Total marks for this page ☐

Investigating paper towels

1

Sharon did a test to see how much water different brands of paper towel soaked up. She hung strips of towel into some water. She measured how far up the water soaked.

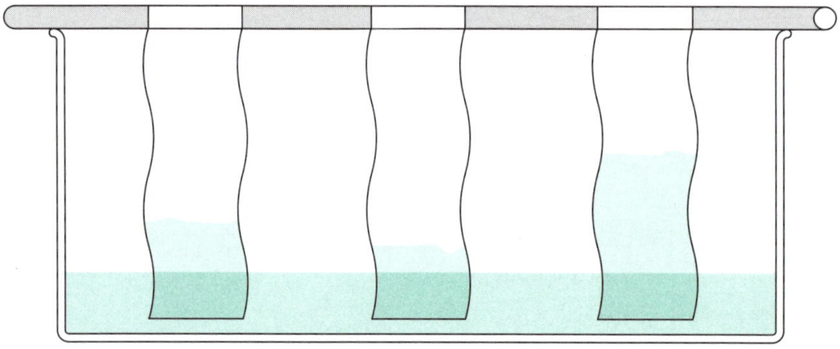

a) Which question was she investigating?
Tick one box.

Which strip was strongest? ☐

Which towel was best value for money? ☐

Which towel absorbed most water? ☐

Which towel would last longest? ☐

1a
1 mark

She recorded her results.

Type of towel	Distance water soaked up towel in 30 seconds (cm)
Quickee mart	4
Sumbodys	5
Tosca	3

b) Which towel was best at soaking up water quickly?

1b
1 mark

c) Explain your idea.

1c
2 marks

d) What was she changing?
Tick one box.

The amount of water. ☐

The type of towel. ☐

The time she left it in water. ☐

1 mark 1d

e) What did she measure?
Tick one box.

The weight of water. ☐

The distance up the towel. ☐

1 mark 1e

f) What did she always keep the same?
Tick one box.

The time she left them. ☐

The amount they soaked up. ☐

The height it went up the towel. ☐

1 mark 1f

Sharon could have done the test in a different way.
She wondered about using a water dropper.

g) Give one suggestion for another way to do this sort of test.

2 marks 1g

Total marks for this page

Plant parts

1 What is the job of plant roots?

1 — 1 mark

2 What is the job of a plant's flower?
Tick one box.

Look pretty. ☐

Feed pollen and nectar to bees. ☐

Make seeds. ☐

2 — 1 mark

3 What is the job of a plant's stem?

3 — 1 mark

4 What purpose do seeds have?

4 — 1 mark

5 What do leaves have to do?
Tick one box.

Provide shade. ☐

Make food for the plant. ☐

Provide food and shelter for small animals. ☐

5 — 1 mark

Total marks for this page

Flower parts

1 This diagram shows the different parts of a flower. Name the parts a–d.

3 marks 1

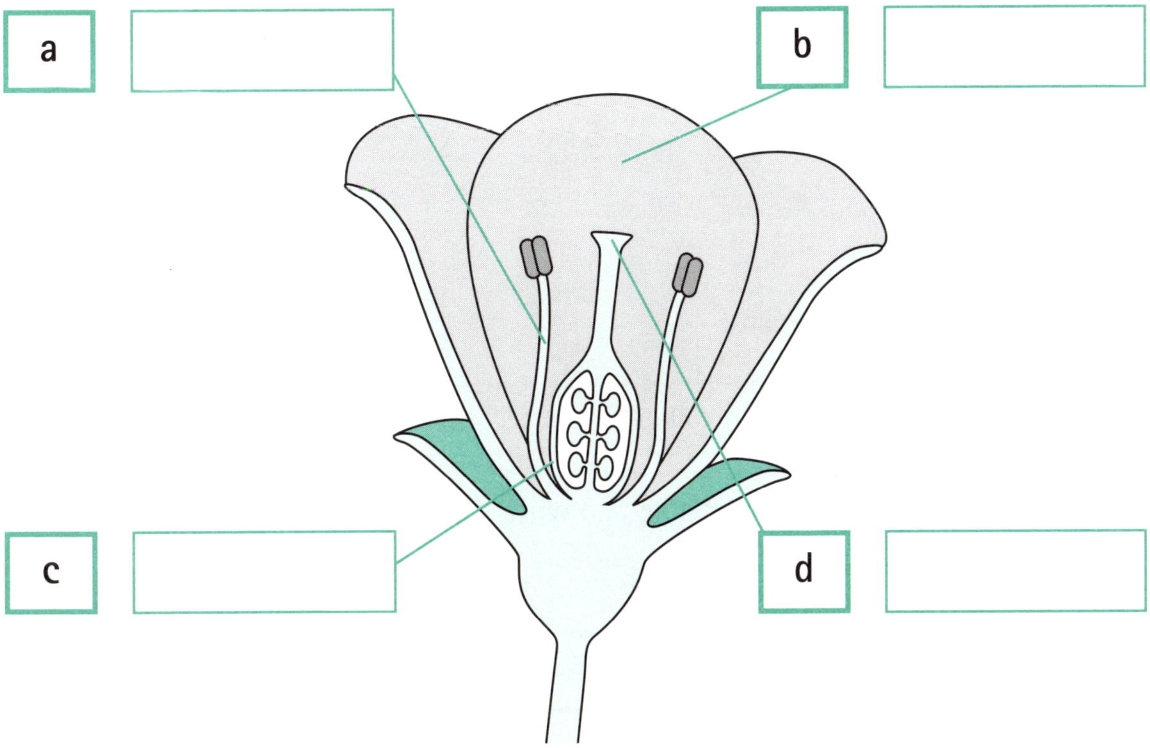

2 This diagram shows a cross-section of the different parts of the flower. Name the parts a, b and c.

3 marks 2

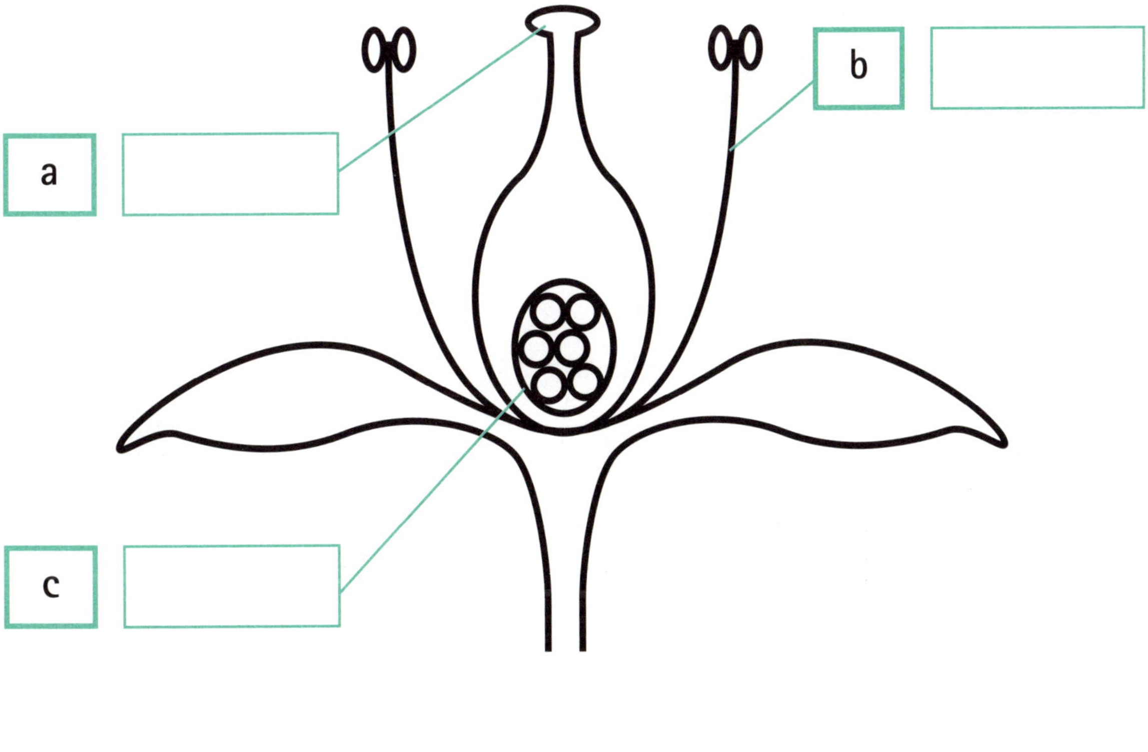

Total marks for this page

Human organs

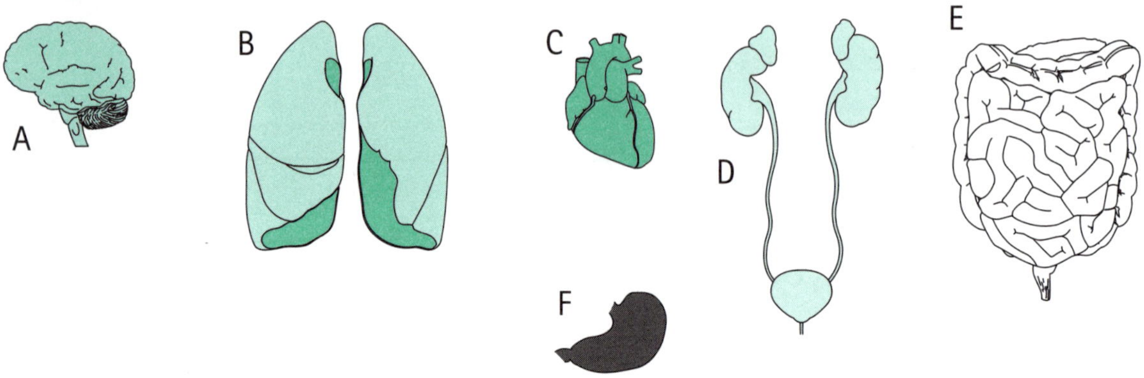

1. The drawings are of some human organs.

stomach	intestines	bladder and kidneys	heart	lungs	brain

Match each picture to the correct organ name and write it in the box below.

A

B

C

D

E

F

1 — 3 marks

2. Draw the organs in the right place on the body.

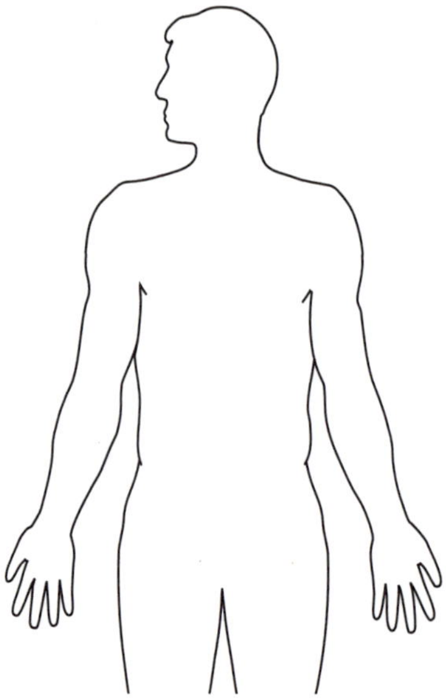

2 — 3 marks

Total marks for this page

Living processes

1. How do you know that a mouse is alive?
List as many reasons as you can.

1 3 marks

2. Imagine you had a pet mouse.
List some of the things you would do to keep it alive and well.

2 2 marks

3. How do you know that an oak tree is alive?
List as many reasons as you can.

3 3 marks

4. Imagine you have an acorn and start to grow it indoors.
It must grow to 20 cm tall before you can plant it out.
What would you have to do to make sure it grows into a small tree?

4 3 marks

Total marks for this page

Classification

1 Write the names of these animals in the correct groups below.

pigeon **rat** **bee** **blackbird** **turtle** **butterfly**

mammal (hairy with four legs)	bird (feathers with two legs)
reptile (scaly skin)	insect (six legs)

1

3 marks

2 All these animals have got bony skeletons.
This is the skeleton of an animal.

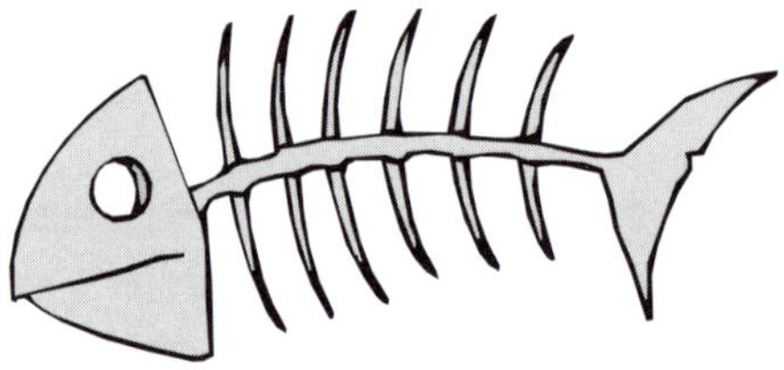

a) To which group of animals does this skeleton belong?

2a

1 mark

b) What is special about this group of animals?
Write one thing.

2b

1 mark

Total marks for this page

Keys

1 a) Put these animals in the correct boxes.

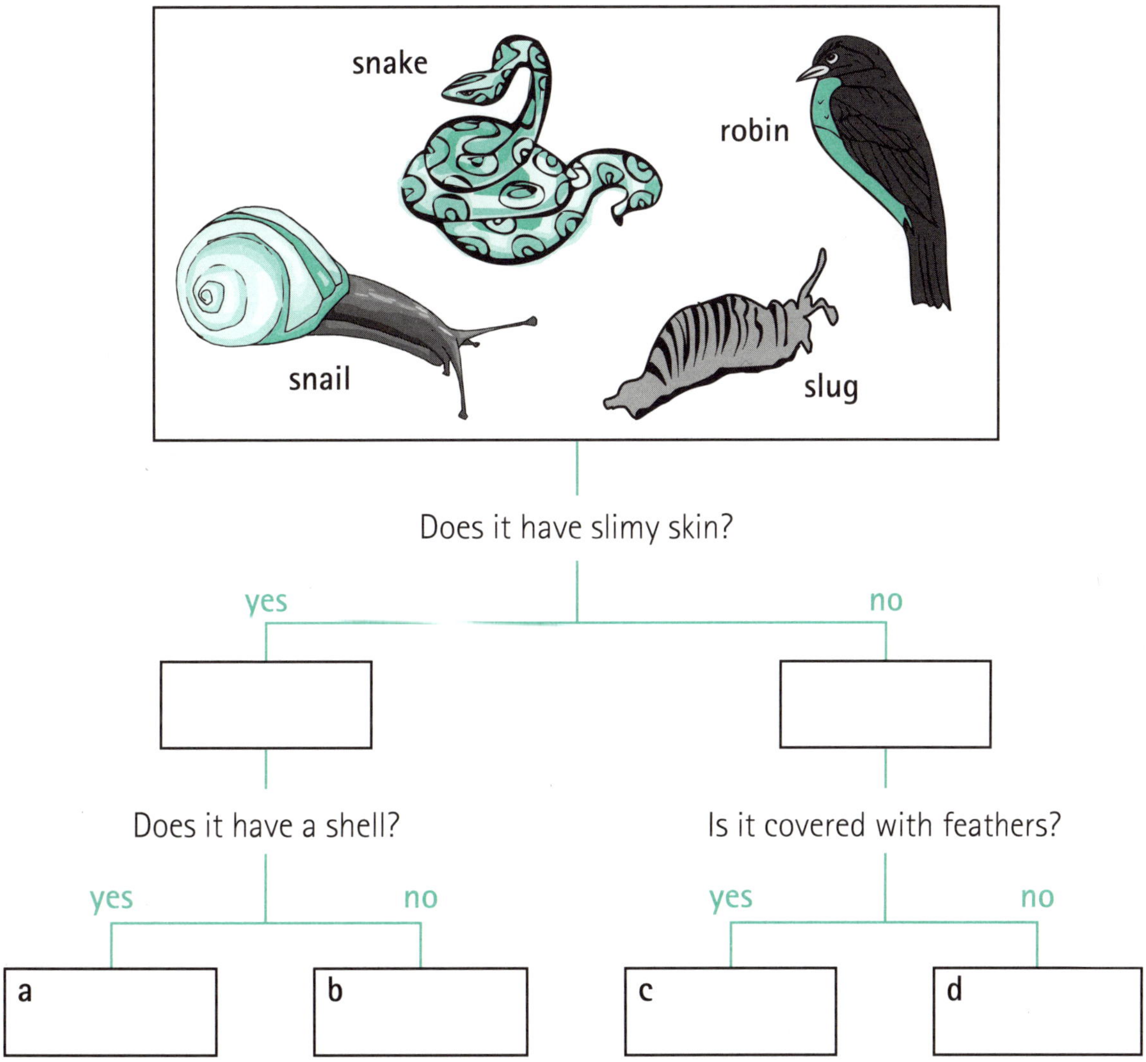

1a — 2 marks

b) Name one other animal that could also go into box c.

1b — 1 mark

c) Name one other animal that could also go into box d.

1c — 1 mark

d) Which group of animals does the snake belong to?

1d — 1 mark

Total marks for this page

Plants and animals in their environment

1

Cactuses live in deserts.
They are adapted to hot dry places.

How is a cactus adapted to life in the desert?
Write an explanation of the adaptation in each box.

spines

thick covering

deep roots

1
3 marks

2

Why do desert rats live underground during the day and only come out at night?

2
1 mark

3

Draw a line from the animal to where it lives.
Connect where it lives to the adaptation.

ANIMAL	WHERE IT LIVES	ADAPTATION
chimp	underground	strong arms to grasp tree branches
shark	jungle	long thin body coated with slime
earthworm	in the sea	hump of fat on back and able to store water in stomach
pet dog	in deserts	helps protect and is loyal to owner
camel	in houses	has a streamlined body and sharp teeth

3
3 marks

Total marks for this page

Predators and prey

1 Draw an arrow from the prey to the predator.

Prey	Predator
worm	house cat
zebra	water beetle
rabbit	blackbird
tadpole	lion
sparrow	fox

1 3 marks

2 Look at these three food chains.

grass ⇒ antelope ⇒ lion

leaves ⇒ caterpillar ⇒ blue tit ⇒ hawk

pond weed ⇒ tadpole ⇒ beetle ⇒ fish

What sort of living thing does each begin with?

2 1 mark

3 Think about food chains you know.

Write your own food chains like those in question 2.

a) ⇒ ⇒

b) ⇒ ⇒

c) ⇒ ⇒

3 3 marks

Total marks for this page

Human food chains

1 This is the food chain for chicken.

Sun ⇒ seeds ⇒ chicken ⇒ person

a) Draw in the arrows in this food chain.

Sun [ ] oak tree (acorns) [ ] pig [ ] person

[ ] 1a
1 mark

b) Write in the missing word in this food chain.

Sun ⇒ [ ] ⇒ cow ⇒ person

[ ] 1b
1 mark

c) Write a food chain for orange juice.

Sun ⇒ [ ] ⇒ person

[ ] 1c
1 mark

2 Humans like to eat fish like cod. Draw a food chain for cod.
It should include these things:

cod	seaweed	small fish	person	shrimps

[ ]

[ ] 2
1 mark

3 This food chain exists in Antarctica.
Fill in the blank with one of these animals.

penguin	blue whale	polar bear

plant plankton ⇒ animal plankton ⇒ small shrimps ⇒ fish ⇒

[ ] ⇒ sea lions ⇒ killer whales

[ ] 3
1 mark

Total marks for this page [ ]

Odd one out

1 Circle the odd one out for each of these groups.
The first one has been done for you.

cow horse chicken

Chicken is a bird. The other two are mammals.

a) horse crocodile sheep

[ ] is a [ ] The other two are [ ]

1a
2 marks

b) robin dragonfly starling

[ ] is an [ ] The other two are [ ]

1b
2 marks

c) sticklcback shark seal

[ ] is a [ ] The other two are [ ]

1c
2 marks

d) shark whale seal

[ ] is a [ ] The other two are [ ]

1d
2 marks

e) human sheep lizard

[ ] is a [ ] The other two are [ ]

1e
2 marks

Total marks for this page

Heat insulators and conductors

1

Choose the best material for the job.
Tick one box in each list.

a) Metal is the best material for a radiator because it is

a good insulator ☐

a good heat conductor ☐

1a — 1 mark

b) Plastic is the best material for a pan handle because it is

a good insulator ☐

a good heat conductor ☐

1b — 1 mark

2

Jo has filled three cups with hot water. One cup is polystyrene, one is pottery and one is metal. She put a temperature sensor in each cup.

The graph looks like this.

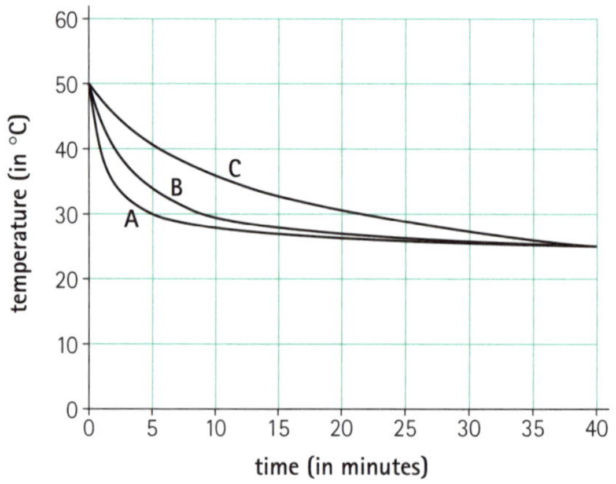

Match the cup to the sensor line.

polystyrene cup	Sensor Line A
metal cup	Sensor Line B
pottery cup	Sensor Line C

2 — 1 mark

3

Jim held ice cube A in his bare hand and ice cube B in a gloved hand.

a) Which cube will melt most quickly?

3a — 1 mark

b) Explain your idea.

3b — 2 marks

Total marks for this page

Gases

1 Label this drawing with the words in the box.

solid	liquid	gas

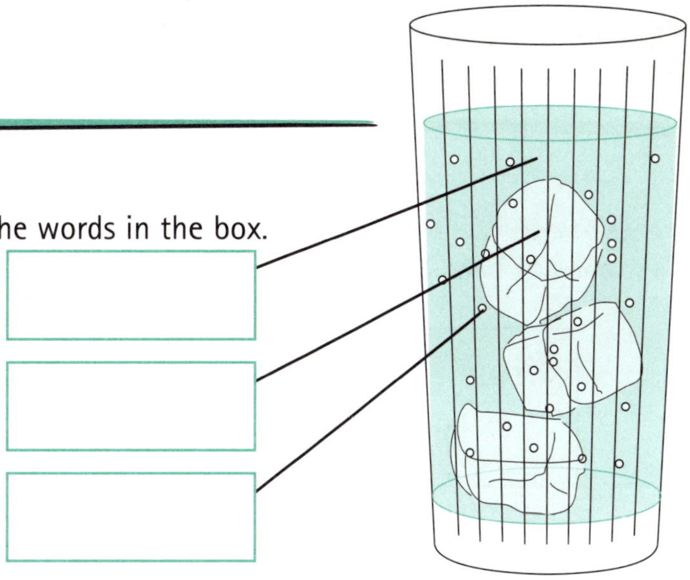

1 mark

2 Complete these sentences.

a) When water evaporates it turns from a liquid to a

2a 1 mark

b) When water condenses it turns from a gas to a

2b 1 mark

c) When water freezes it turns from a liquid to a

2c 1 mark

3 Connect the substance to the correct state.
All are at room temperature.

oxygen
water
wax
chocolate
steel
carbon dioxide
mercury (metal)
alcohol

SOLID

LIQUID

GAS

3 marks

Total marks for this page

Grouping materials

1 Harry put these materials into a branching key. Write the names into each box. The first one has been done for you.

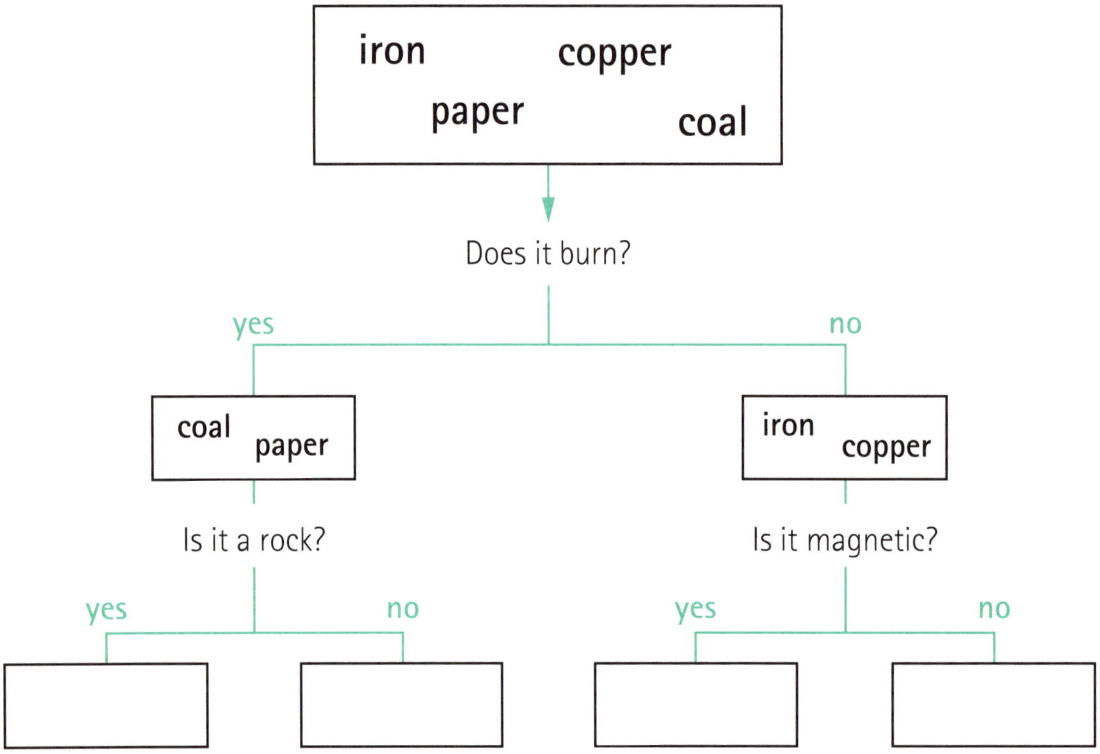

1
2 marks

2 Choose three materials. Now try a branching key of your own. One of the bottom boxes will be empty.

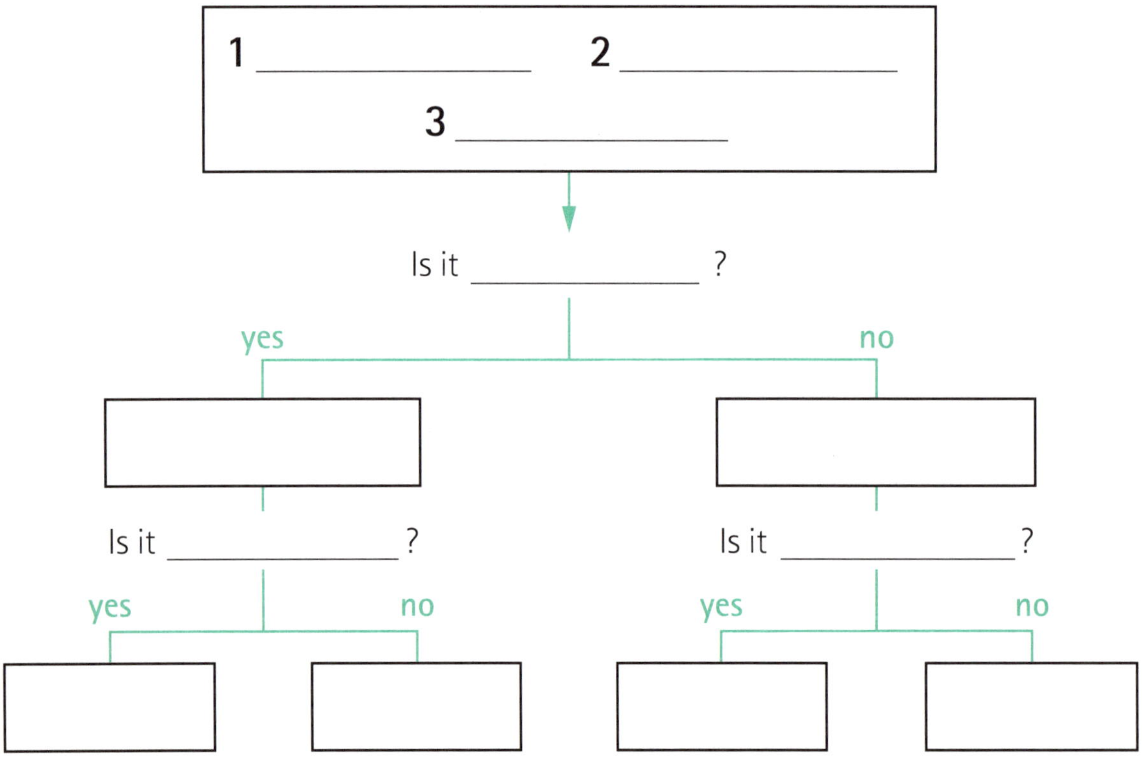

2
2 marks

Total marks for this page

Separating mixtures

1 Draw a line from the mixture to the best way to separate it.

salt and water	filtering
sand and iron filings	sieving
sand and water	using a magnet
pebbles from soil	letting the liquid evaporate

1 2 marks

2 Max has a mixture of salt, tiny polystyrene balls and sand.
Suggest how he could separate them.
He will need three steps.

First he could...	Then he could...	Finally...

2 3 marks

3 Samantha has a mixture of tiny stones, sand and sugar.
Suggest how she could separate them.
She will need three steps.

First she could...	Next...	Lastly...

3 3 marks

Total marks for this page

Making mixtures

1

Tim mixed four solids with water.
Tick the boxes of those solids which dissolved.

☐	salt	after a minute the mixture was see-through
☐	soil	all the soil sunk to the bottom
☐	plaster of Paris	the mixture was cloudy then went stiff
☐	jelly	the mixture was see-through and red coloured

1 2 marks

2

Plaster of Paris is a powder.
When it is mixed with water it goes creamy.
Then it sets to become a solid.

a) Predict whether you think this change is reversible.
Tick one box.

I think the change is reversible. ☐

I think the change is not reversible. ☐

2a 1 mark

b) Explain your idea.

2b 2 marks

3

Cement also goes hard after mixing with water.
Give one reason you know that this change is not reversible.

3 1 mark

Total marks for this page

Force arrows

1 The boot is pushing the ball in the direction of the arrow.

Draw an arrow to show the direction of push on the tennis ball.

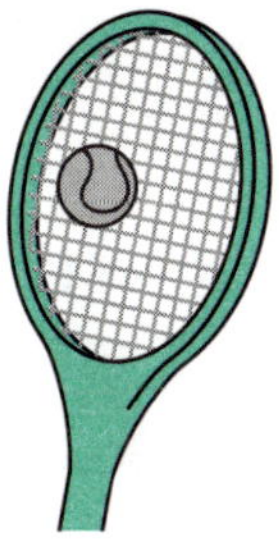

1 mark 1

2 The bike is rolling to a stop.
The force from the brakes is slowing it down.

This car is slowing down with its brakes.
Draw an arrow to show the direction of the force.

1 mark 2

3 The force of gravity is pulling on the case.

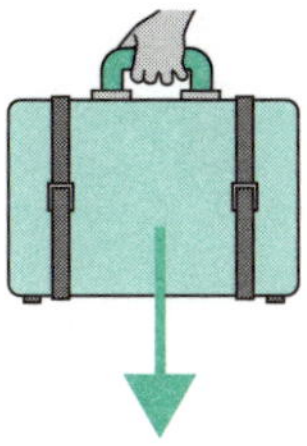

Draw the pull of gravity on this heavy watering can.

1 mark 3

4 Draw arrows to show the force of gravity.

1 mark 4

5 This car is speeding up as it rolls down the slope.
Draw an arrow to show the direction of the force.

1 mark 5

6 This car is slowing as it rolls up the slope.
Draw an arrow to show the direction of the force.

1 mark 6

7 This parachute is falling through the air.
Draw an arrow to show the direction of the air resistance on it.

1 mark 7

8 This human cannonball is rushing through the air.
Draw an arrow to show the direction of the air resistance on him.

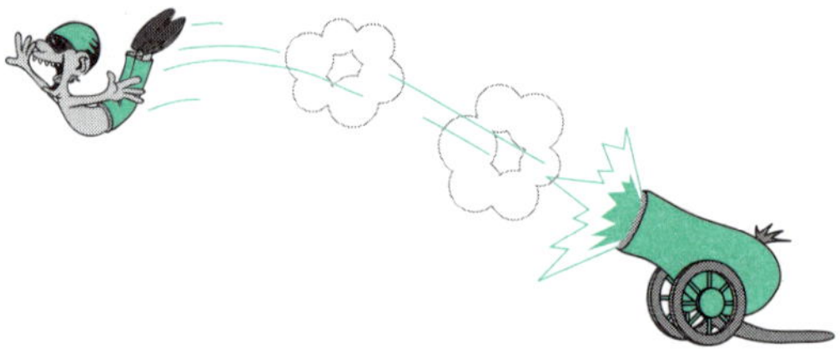

1 mark 8

9

a) This submarine is diving. Draw an arrow to show the direction of the force.

b) This submarine is rising. Draw an arrow to show the direction of the force.

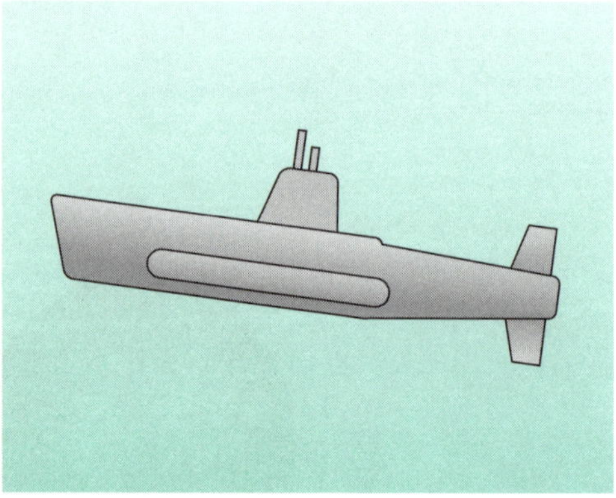

2 marks 9

Total marks for this page

Magnetic attraction and repulsion

1 Draw the direction of the force on the paperclip.

1 mark 1

2 Draw arrows to show the direction of the force between these north and south poles.

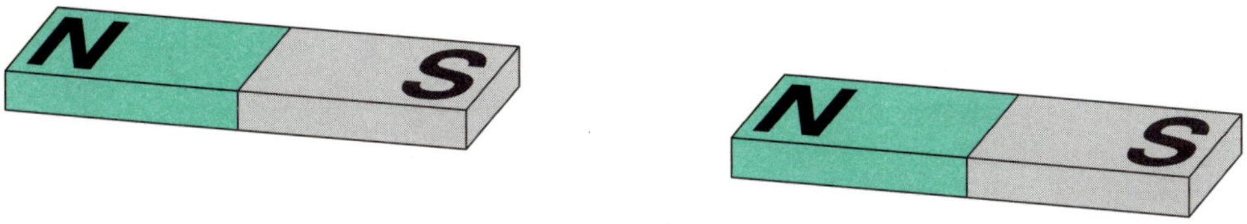

1 mark 2

3 Draw arrows to show the direction of the force between these north poles.

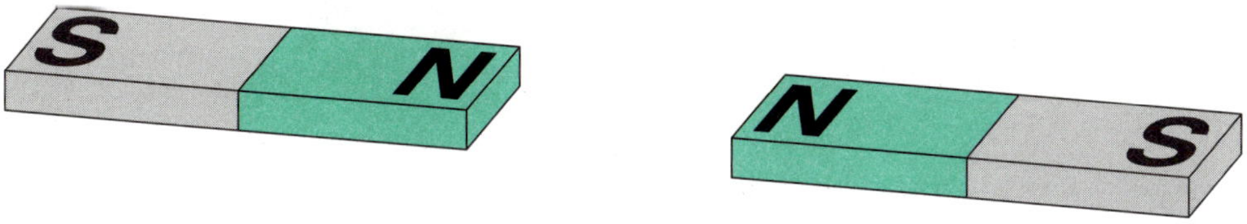

1 mark 3

4 Paula thinks that magnets do not work through some materials.
Kate thinks magnets work through all materials.

a) Describe how you could test if magnetic force worked through air.

1 mark 4a

b) Describe how you could test if magnetic force worked through wood.

1 mark 4b

Total marks for this page

Electrical circuits

1 Katie made a question and answer board.
She connected it like this.

She touches the wire on the paper clips next to 12 and 4 × 3.
Explain why the bulb lights.

[ ]

[ ] 2 marks 1

2 Jim connected a motor into four circuits.
Tick the box next to the circuits that will work.

a)

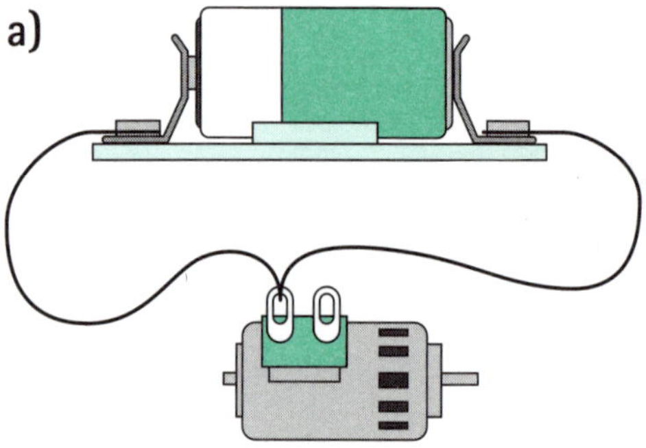

[ ]

b)

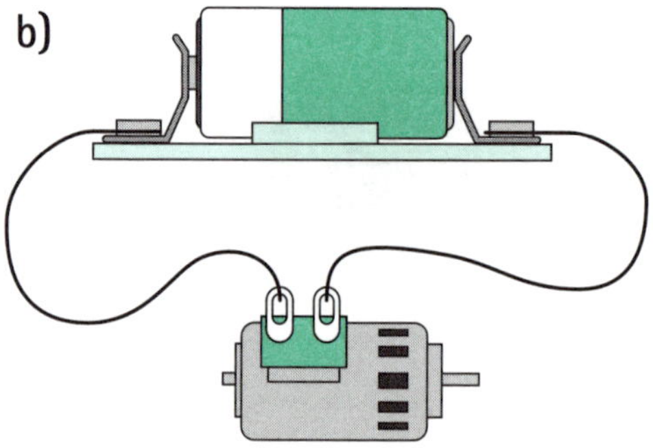

[ ]

c)

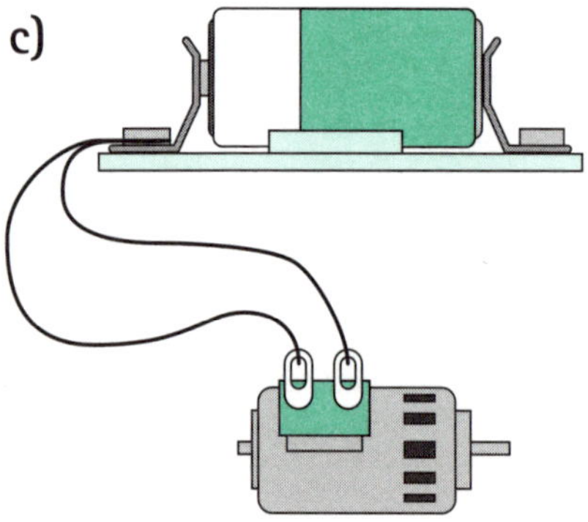

[ ]

d)

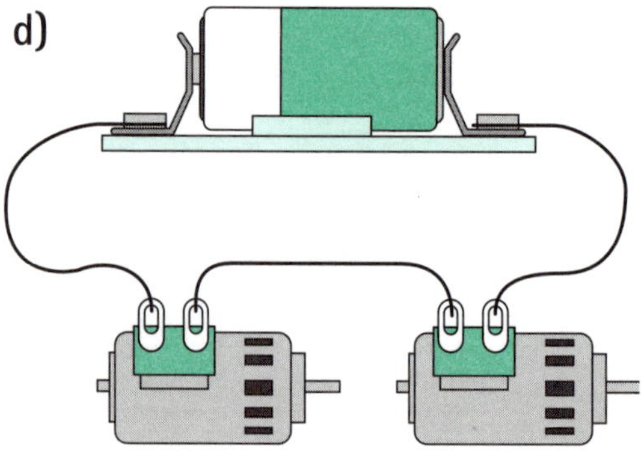

[ ]

[ ] 2 marks 2

Total marks for this page [ ]

Electrical switches

Switches can be open or closed.

This switch is open. **This switch is closed.**

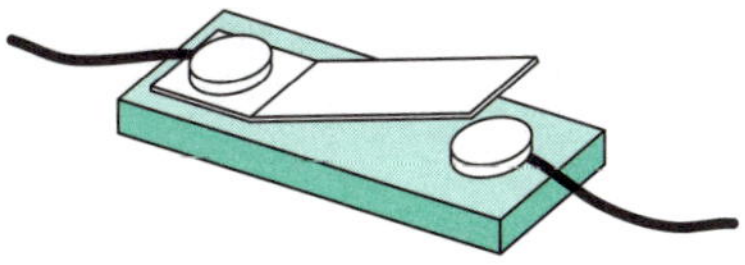

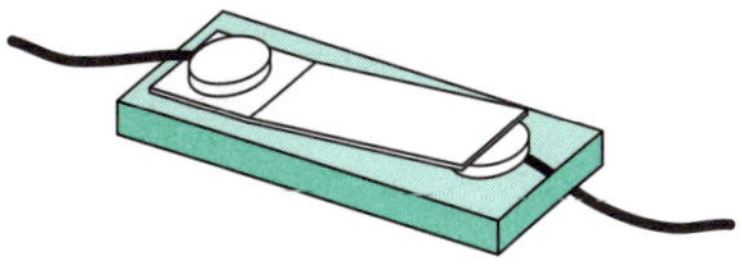

(1) Fran has made a circuit with a bulb, battery and switch.
The switch is open.
Is the bulb glowing?

YES ☐

NO ☐

☐ 1
1 mark

(2) Fran has made a circuit with a motor, battery and switch.
The switch is open.
Is the motor spinning?

YES ☐

NO ☐

☐ 2
1 mark

(3) Karen connected a switch into two circuits.

a) Tick the box under the circuit where the buzzer is sounding.

A

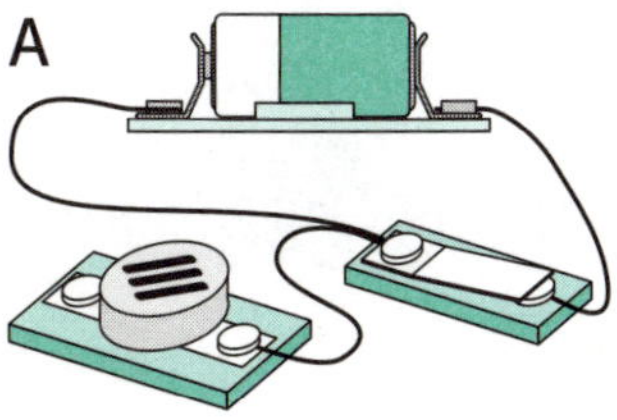

☐

B

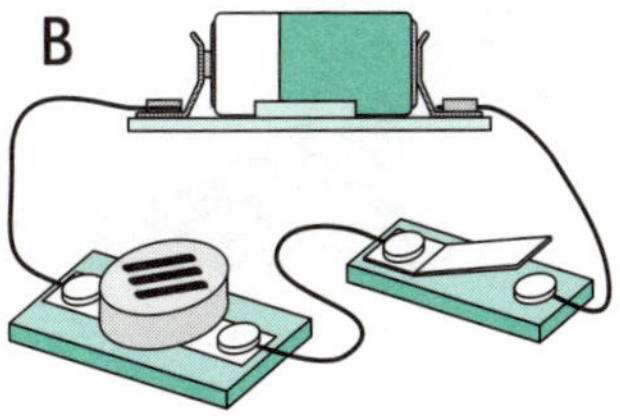

☐

C

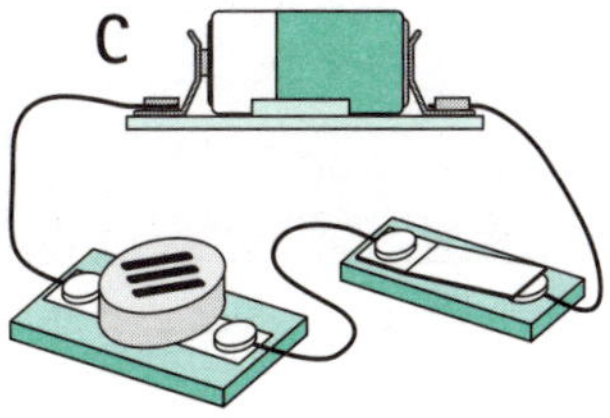

☐

☐ 3a
1 mark

b) Explain why you have ticked your chosen circuit.

☐ 3b
2 marks

Total marks for this page ☐

The position of the Sun

1

It is winter.
Draw a line to match each time of day to the position of the Sun.

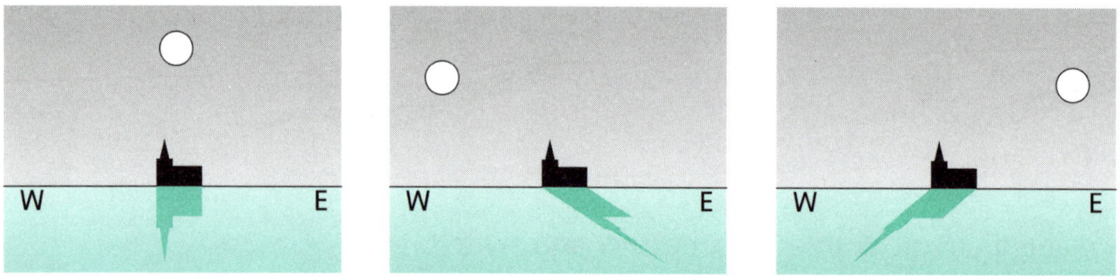

8 o'clock in the morning   noon   4 o'clock in the afternoon

1a
1 mark

The Moon

2

a) Write the correct name under each phase of the Moon.
Choose from:

full	new	crescent	half	gibbous

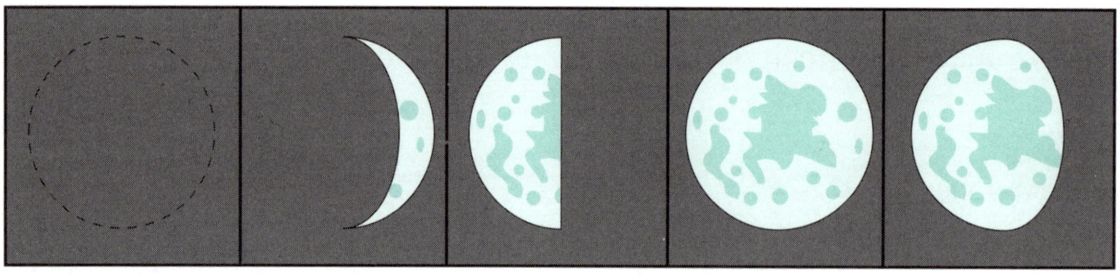

2a
2 marks

b) Pete thinks the Moon is a source of light.
Fay thinks it is only reflecting the Sun's light.
Who do you think is right?

________________ is right.

2b
1 mark

Total marks for this page

Air resistance

1

Bob drops two parachutes.
One is large. The other is small.
Both are made from old plastic bags.
Both have the same weights on the end.

Which one do you think will hit the ground first?
Explain your idea.

1 — 1 mark

2

Draw arrows to show the air resistance force on both parachutes.

2 — 1 mark

3

Tina measures the distance that her toy car rolls off a ramp.
She tapes a piece of card on the car.
She measures how far it goes with cards of different size.

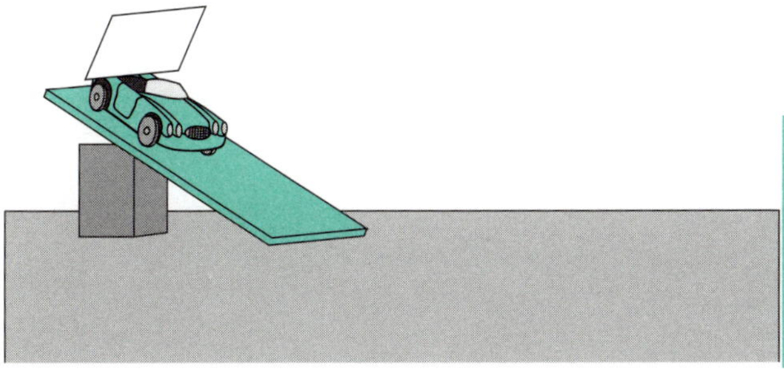

Size of card	Distance rolled
small	60cm
medium	54cm
large	50cm

What pattern do you notice?

3 — 1 mark

4

Explain why the size of the card affects the distance the car rolls.

4 — 2 marks

Total marks for this page

Friction force

Fran put four objects on a tray.
She slowly tipped it up.

The pencil sharpener slid first.
The matchbox slid next.
The scissors slid third.
The rubber slid last.

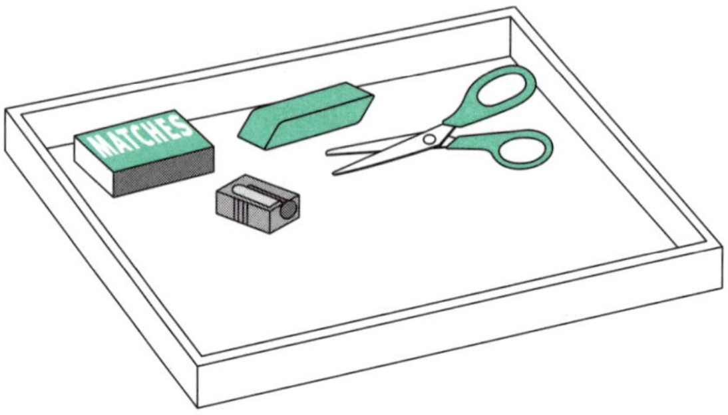

1 Which object has most friction between it and the tray?
Use the information above to help you.
Tick one box.

rubber ☐ matchbox ☐

scissors ☐ pencil sharpener ☐

1 mark 1

2 Which object has least friction between it and the tray?
Tick one box.

rubber ☐ matchbox ☐

scissors ☐ pencil sharpener ☐

1 mark 2

3 Fran put a piece of carpet on the tray.
Tick one box.

This will increase the friction. ☐

This will make the friction less. ☐

1 mark 3

4 Fran pulled a box across the carpet.
She used a spring balance to measure the force.
She put masses in the box.
She measured the force needed to pull again.

a) What force was she measuring?

1 mark 4a

b) Which unit did she use to measure the force?

1 mark 4b

Total marks for this page

Using sensors for light and sound

Class 5 used a sensor to record light levels.
They recorded the light in their classroom over one day.
This is the graph they printed.

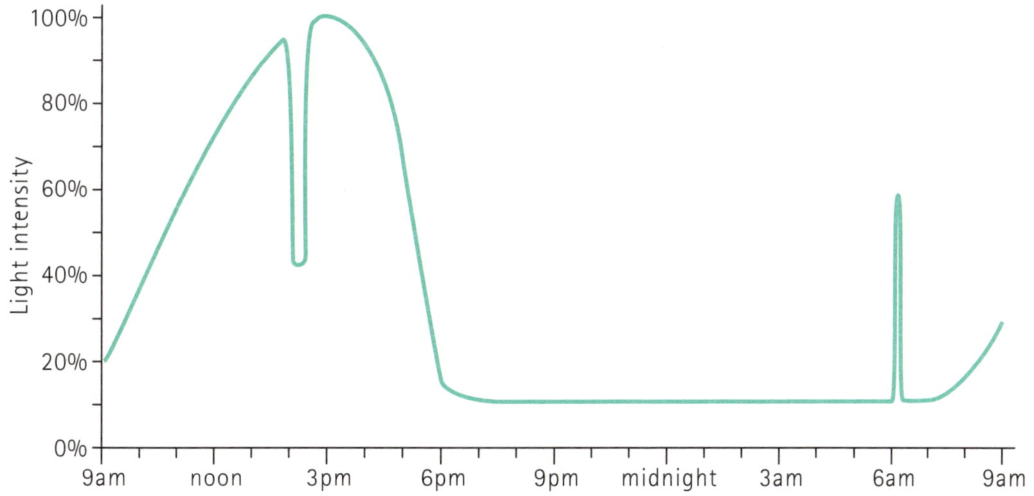

1 **a)** There was a sudden increase in light at 6 o'clock in the morning. What might have caused it?

1a — 1 mark

b) At which time in the morning did the Sun begin to rise?

Tick one box.

6 o'clock ☐ 7 o'clock ☐ 9 o'clock ☐

1b — 1 mark

2 At 2pm the class watched a TV programme.

a) What happened to the light in the classroom at that time?

2a — 1 mark

b) Try to explain why this happened.

2b — 1 mark

3

The class tested which sunglasses let through most light.
They tested three kinds.
They held each over the sensor.
This is the graph they made.

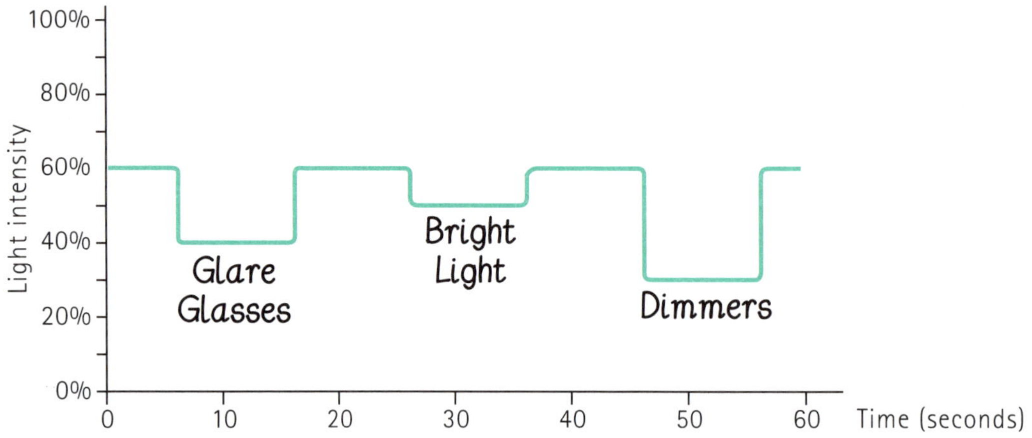

a) Which of the sunglasses let through most light?

3a 1 mark

b) Which ones let through least light?

3b 1 mark

4

The class wanted to test which cloth would make the best blackout curtains.
They only had a small sample of each.
How could they use their light sensor to test the samples?

4 2 marks

5

The class used a sound sensor in the computer.
Suggest a question they could investigate with the sound sensor.

5 1 mark

Total marks for this page

Sounds through different materials

Dolphins and bats both use echoes to find their food.
Snakes listen to vibrations through the ground.

1 Which materials can sound travel through?
Tick those through which sound can travel.

air ☐ water ☐ rock ☐

1 — 1 mark

2 There is a long steel handrail in the playground.
Sarah stands at one end and John at the other.
Sarah asks John to tap it gently.
She can hardly hear him.

a) What is the sound travelling through to reach her ear?

2a — 1 mark

She puts her ear to the rail.
She can hear much better now.

b) Do sounds travel better through solids or gas?

2b — 1 mark

c) Explain your answer.

2c — 1 mark

3 Children in Class 2 are having fun with string telephones.
Explain how they work.

3 — 2 marks

Total marks for this page

Shadows

1 Javed is looking at his birthday candles.

a) Draw an arrow to show how he sees them.

1a 1 mark

b) Javed makes a shadow of a toy using his torch.
The shadow falls on the wall.
Tick the correct box.

The shadow is a reflection of the toy. ☐

The shadow is made where the light is blocked. ☐

The shadow forms because the toy is translucent (you can see through it). ☐

1b 1 mark

2 Javed kept the toy in the same place.
He started with the torch close to the toy.
He moved the torch further away from the toy.
These are his results.

Distance from toy	Height of shadow
25 cm	12 cm
50 cm	10 cm
75 cm	9 cm

What happens to the size of the shadow as the torch moves further away?
Tick one box.

It gets smaller. ☐

It stays the same. ☐

It gets bigger. ☐

2 1 mark

3 **a)** In his investigation which factor did Javed vary?

The variable he measured was ______

3a 1 mark

b) In his investigation what was one of the variables that Javed kept the same?

One of the variables he kept the same was ______

3b 1 mark

Total marks for this page

KEY FACTS - Sc1

At Level 3 you need to be able to:

- put forward your own ideas to answer a question
- know why it is important to gather data to answer questions
- make observations
- use simple measuring equipment
- carry out a fair test with help
- record observations in a variety of ways
- explain observations
- suggest improvements to your work

At Level 4 you need to be able to:

- see that you need evidence to support scientific ideas
- decide on the best way to do an experiment or test
- make good predictions
- select the most important information
- choose the best equipment for a test
- record observations and measurements
- draw and make sense of a bar chart
- come to conclusions
- say ways in which work can be improved

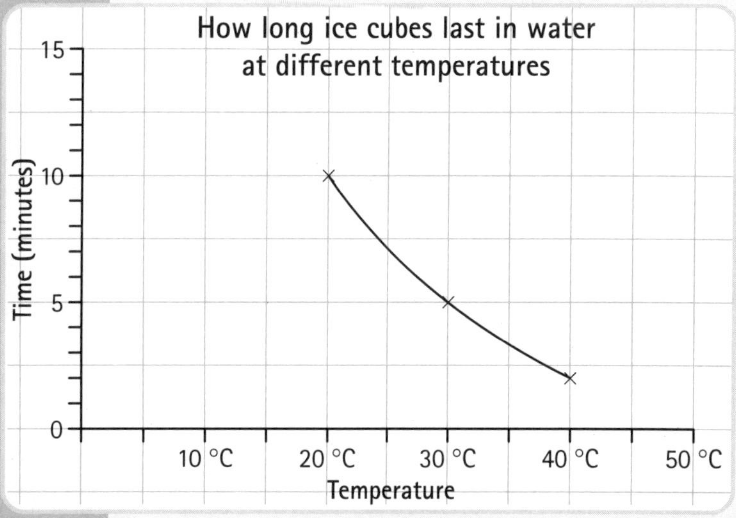

KEY FACTS – Sc2

At Level 3 you need to know:

- about basic life processes
- the differences between living and non-living things
- reasons for changes in living things, such as diet and water supply
- the ways in which animals are suited to their environment

At Level 4 you need to know:

- the names of some of the organs of the human body
- the position of some of the organs of the human body
- the names and position of some of the organs of a variety of plants
- how to use simple keys to identify living things
- how to put living things into groups
- about food chains

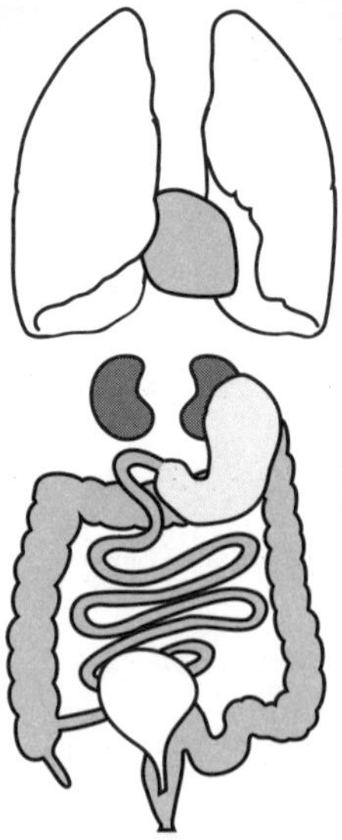

KEY FACTS – Sc3

At Level 3 you need to know:

- how to put forward your own ideas to answer a question
- about sorting materials into groups
- why some materials are suited to a particular purpose
- which changes can be reversed
- which changes cannot be reversed

At Level 4 you need to know:

- that you need evidence to support scientific ideas
- about the properties of materials
- how materials are classified into solids, liquids and gases
- how to separate simple mixtures
- the scientific words used to describe changes, such as condense, evaporate and freeze
- which changes are easily reversed and which changes are difficult to reverse

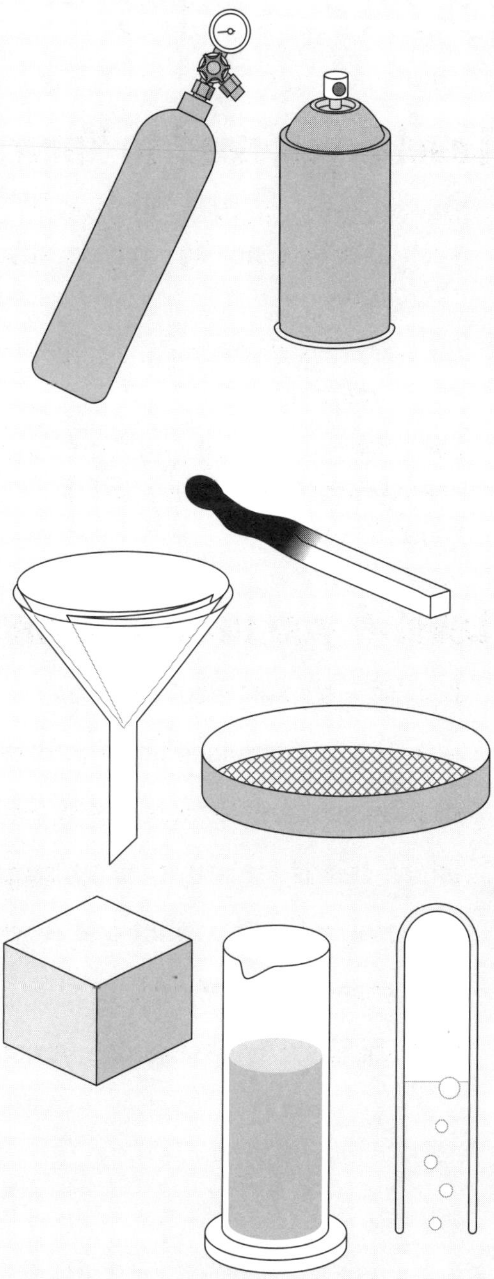

KEY FACTS – Sc4

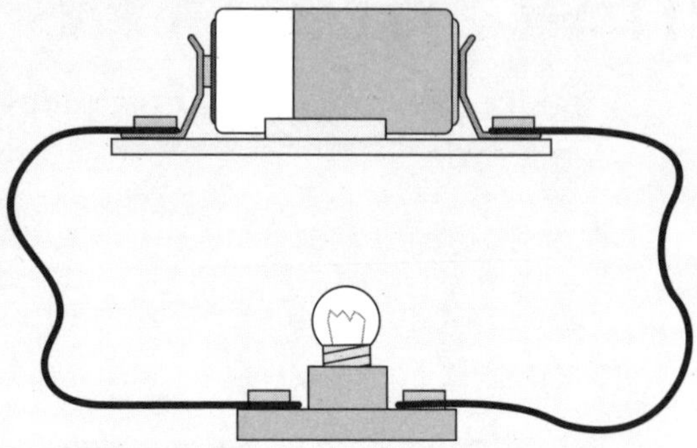

At Level 3 you need to know:

- the causes and effects in physical processes, such as a bulb not lighting because of a break in the circuit
- about forces changing the direction or speed of movement
- the effects of sound and light, such as the way they get fainter as the sources become more distant

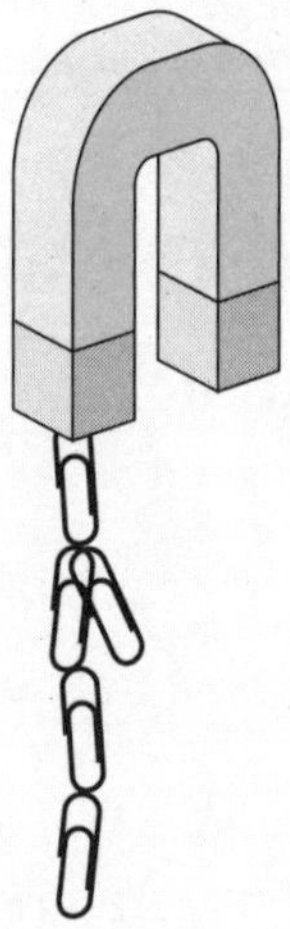

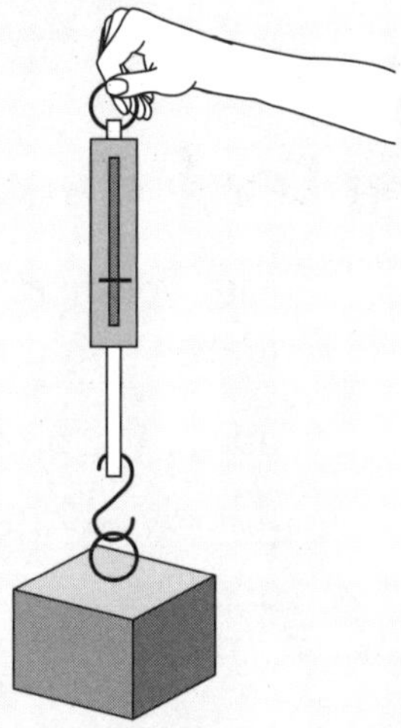

At Level 4 you need to know:

- how to alter electrical circuits
- how the Sun changes position during the day
- that objects are attracted by gravity
- which things are attracted by magnets
- that magnets can attract and repel each other
- how shadows are formed
- that sounds travel through a variety of materials

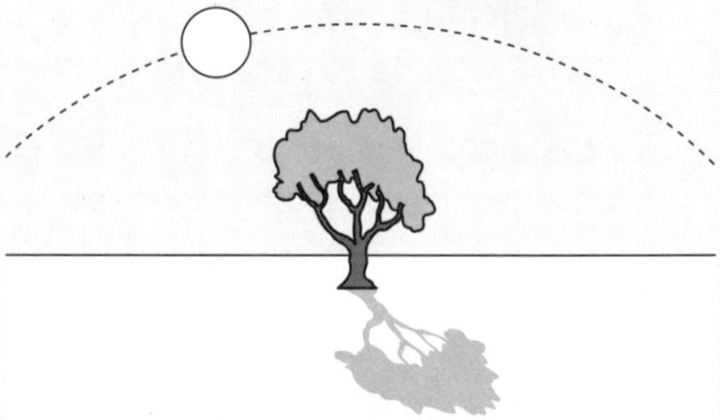

Answers

Page 10

1 Thermometer
2 Long tape measure
3 Answers will vary but you should carry out the same test on each type of cloth, e.g. test the strength of each material by hanging weights from it until it tears.
4 Answers will vary but Terry should put it in both damp and dry soil.
5 Sally should connect the batteries to a bulb and see which light is brighter.

Page 11

1 a) 10 cm b) 26 cm
c) The car travelled a shorter distance when the ramp was 5 and 6 blocks steep.
2 Answers will vary but should mention that the further away from the tree the dandelion was the more light it would get and the higher it would grow. It would also get more water.

Page 12

1

2

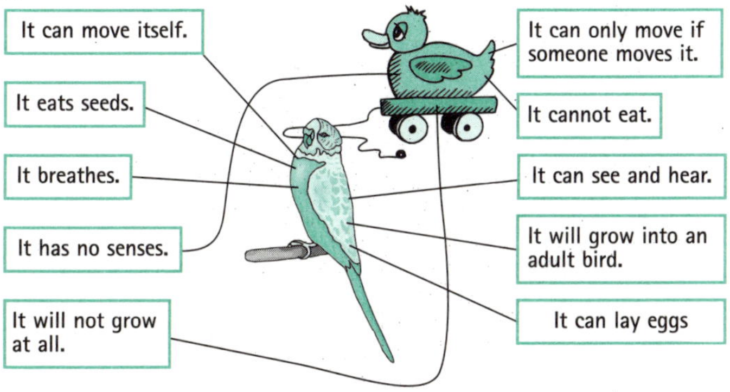

3 Living things grow, feed, breathe, use their senses, get rid of waste, reproduce, move.

Page 13

1 a) Plant C, b) Plant A, c) Where they were growing, the size of the plant pot and the type of compost should remain the same.
2 a) Tick: She put one plant on the windowsill.
Cross: She put one plant in the cupboard.
b) Tick all except Where they were growing.

Page 14

1 Tick: aluminium, steel, lead.
2 Is attracted to a magnet: steel, iron. Is not attracted to a magnet: copper, plastic, glass, lead, aluminium.
3 Floats: wood, polystyrene, wax. Sinks: steel, glass, lead, aluminium.

Page 15

1 Wire is metal (usually copper), insulation is plastic.
2 a) The pins of a plug are metal because metal is an electrical conductor and will let electricity get to the appliance.
b) The back of the plug is plastic because plastic is an electrical insulator and will stop us from electrocuting ourselves.
3

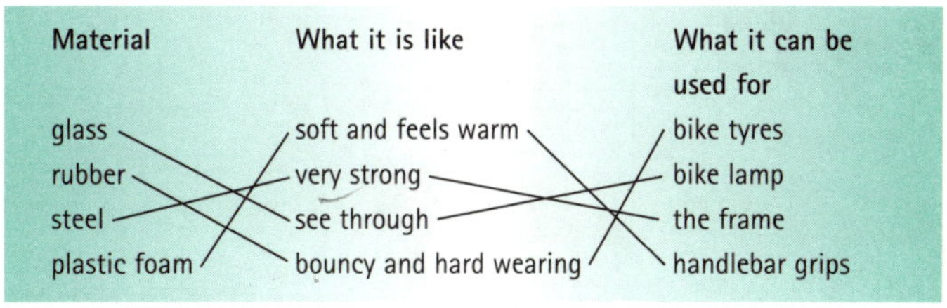

Page 16

1 Answers from top to bottom:
Liquid, Solid, No, Liquid, Solid, Yes
2 Answers from top to bottom: False, True, True, False
3 Pete
4

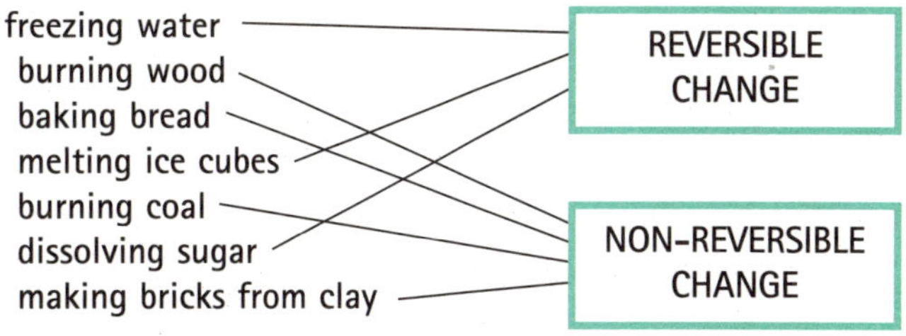

Page 17

1 Tick: The circuit is not complete.
2 The battery has run out.
3 a) The electricity cannot flow through the rubber which is an electrical insulator.
b) The electricity cannot flow because there is a break in the circuit.

Page 18

1 TV, Sun, Torch, Fire, Star – source of light.
Book, Flower – not a source of light.
2 a) Tick the third box.
b) We see because light enters our eyes. The last box shows how the candle casts light in all directions. Some of this light goes into our eyes.

Page 19

1 Tick: Drop bigger objects, Drop objects from higher up, Drop heavier objects.
2 Push the truck faster, start nearer the wall, add weight to the truck.
3 Left to right: 3, 2, 1
4 Left to right, 1, 4, 2, 3

Page 20

1

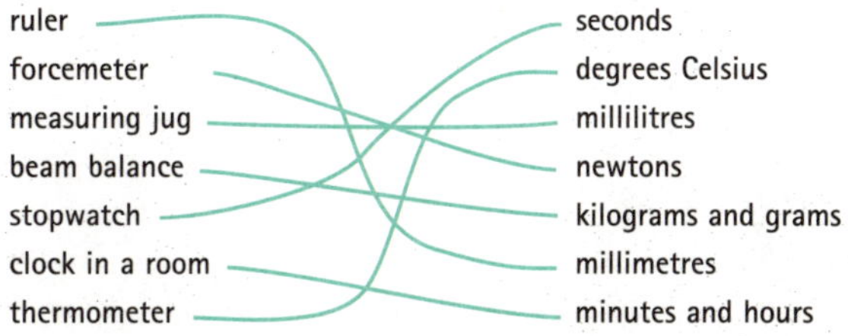

2 Metre ruler
3 Forcemeter/spring balance
4 Stopwatch

Page 21

1 Tick: Do a fair test.
2 Tick: By looking in a tree identification book.
3 Tick: By looking on the internet.
4 Tick: By doing a class survey.

Page 22

1

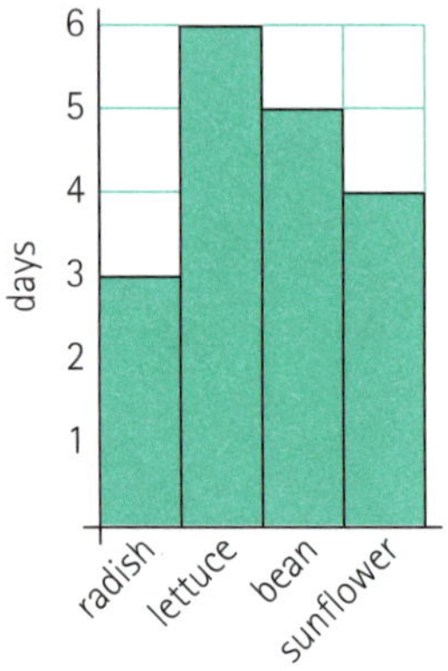

2 From top to bottom: blue, green, brown or green, blue, brown
3

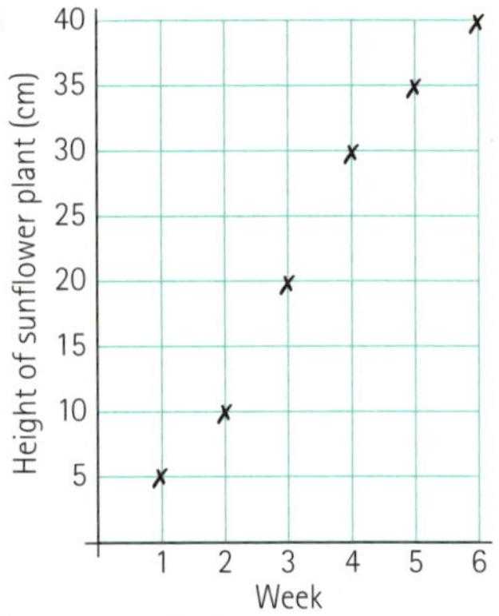

Page 23

1 Most birds were noticed on the school field.
Fewest birds were found on the hedge.
2 10:30am and 12:00 – 12:30pm.
It was break time and lunchtime and children were in the playground.
There were so many birds at 11:00 because break had just ended and the birds had flown to the playground to collect the crisps and biscuits that had been dropped.
3 Sparrow
Garden

Pages 24–25

The answers will vary dependent upon what children choose to investigate.
In the final question the children who drew the chart changed the material that the ice cubes were wrapped in.

Page 26

1 Tick: The thickness of the paper.
2 Tick: Weighs up to 10 newtons.
3 I think the papers will be less strong when they are wet.

Page 27

1 a) Tick: Do large gyrocopters fall slower than smaller ones.
b) Tick: Gyrocopters with longer wings fall slower.
2 a) I would change the number of paper clips on the gyrocopter.
b) I would keep the size of gyrocopter the same and where I dropped it from the same too.

Pages 28–29

1 a) Tick: Which towel absorbed most water?
b) Sumbodys.
c) Answers will vary but should mention that more water was absorbed by Sumbodys because it soaked further up the paper towel.
d) Tick: The type of towel.
e) Tick: The distance up the towel.
f) Tick: The time she left them.
g) Answers will vary, e.g. drop water on the towel until the towel has no dry areas left.

Page 30

1 Roots take water and nutrients from the soil for the plant.
2 Tick: Make seeds.
3 To carry water up from the roots.
4 Seeds grow into new plants.
5 Tick: Make food for the plant.

Page 31

1

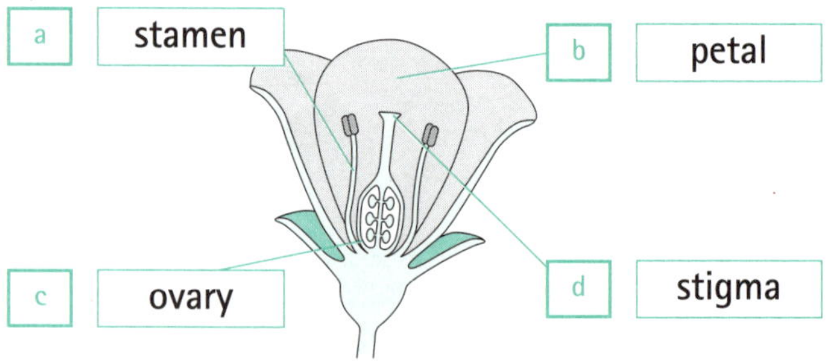

2

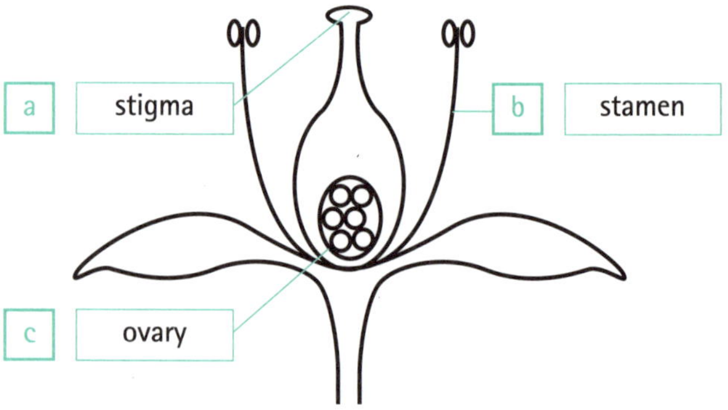

Page 32

1 A) Brain
B) Lungs
C) Heart
D) Bladder and kidneys
E) Intestines
F) Stomach
2

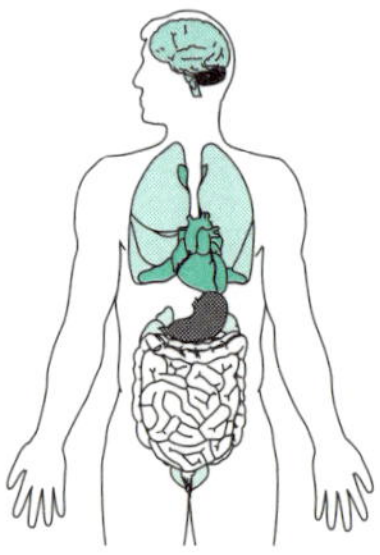

Page 33

1 List: It moves, has babies, has senses, grows, breathes, gets rid of waste and eat.
2 Feed it, give it water, clean up its waste.
3 It produces seeds, it grows, it moves, it gets rid of waste gas (oxygen), it senses where light is, it uses sunlight, water and air to make food.
4 Plant it in soil or compost in a plant pot. Place the pot in the light and give it plenty of water.

Page 34

1 Mammal: rat
Bird: pigeon, blackbird
Reptile: turtle
Insect: bee, butterfly
2 a) Fish
b) They live in water all the time; they breathe through gills.

Page 35

a)

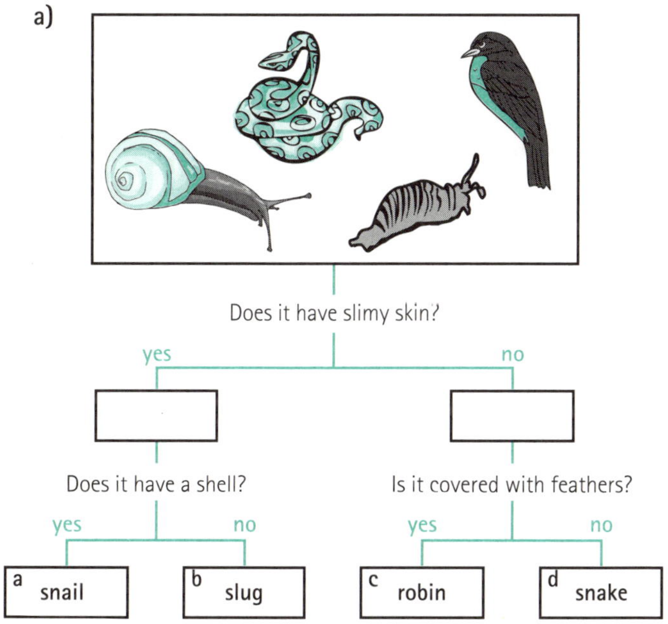

b) Another animal for box c: Pigeon or any bird.
c) Another animal for box d: Any mammal or reptile.
d) A snake is a reptile.

Page 36

1 Spines: stop animals eating the plant.
Thick covering to stop water from evaporating.
Deep roots to get water from the soil.
2 It is cooler underground during the day.
They come out in the cool evening to look for food.
3

ANIMAL	WHERE IT LIVES	ADAPTATION
chimp	jungle	strong arms to grasp tree branches
shark	in the sea	has a streamlined body and sharp teeth
earthworm	underground	long thin body coated with slime
pet dog	in houses	helps protect and is loyal to owner
camel	in deserts	hump of fat on back and able to store water in stomach

Page 37

1

prey	predator
worm	blackbird
zebra	lion
rabbit	fox
tadpole	water beetle
sparrow	house cat

2 A plant
3 Answers will vary but should start with a plant.

Page 38

1 a) Sun → oak tree (acorns) → pig → person. b) Insert 'grass' in food chain. c) Insert 'oranges' in food chain.
2 Seaweed → shrimps → small fish → cod → person.
3 Penguin is the missing word.

Page 39

a) Crocodile is a reptile. The other two are mammals.
b) The dragonfly is an insect. The other two are birds.
c) The seal is a mammal. The other two are fish.
d) The shark is a fish. The other two are mammals.
e) The lizard is a reptile. The other two are mammals.

Page 40

1 a) Tick: a good heat conductor.
b) Tick: a good insulator.
2 Polystyrene cup = sensor line C
Metal cup = sensor line A
Pottery cup = sensor line B
3 a) Ice cube A b) Because the glove insulates the heat from Jim's hand

Page 41

1 From top to bottom: Liquid, Solid, Gas
2 a) Gas, b) liquid, c) solid.
3

Material	State
oxygen	GAS
water	LIQUID
wax	SOLID
chocolate	SOLID
steel	SOLID
carbon dioxide	GAS
mercury (metal)	LIQUID
alcohol	LIQUID

Page 42

1 Boxes from left to right: coal, paper, iron, copper
2 Answers will vary. Get someone to try your key to check that it works.

Page 43

1

Mixture	Method
salt and water	letting the liquid evaporate
sand and iron filings	using a magnet
sand and water	filtering
pebbles from soil	sieving

2 Answers will vary but should include adding water so the poly-styrene balls float and can be removed. The salt will dissolve so you can filter the sand out. Let the water evaporate to get the salt.
3 Answers will vary but should include sieving out the stones, adding water so the sugar dissolves, filtering out the sand, then letting the water evaporate to get the sugar.

Page 44

1 Tick: Salt, Jelly
2 a) Tick: I think the change is not reversible.
   b) The change is not reversible because there has been a chemical reaction and a new material has been made.
3 The change is not reversible because there has been a chemical reaction and a new material has been made.

Pages 45–46

1
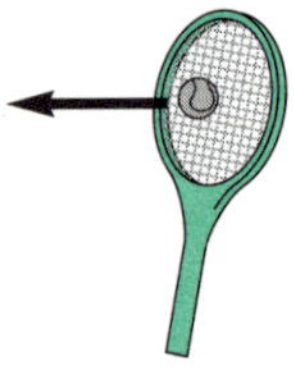

2

3

4

5

6

7

8
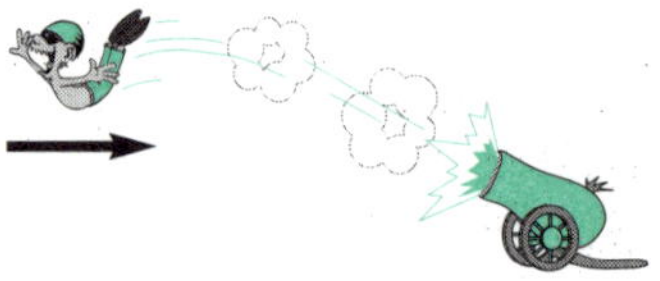

9 a)

b)

Page 47

1
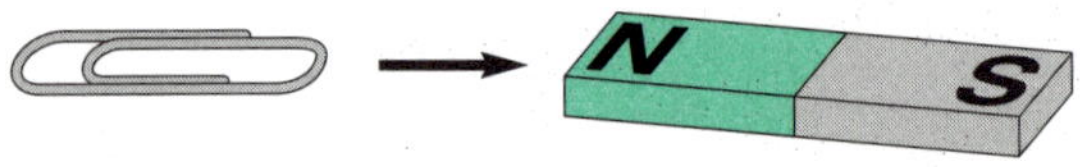

2
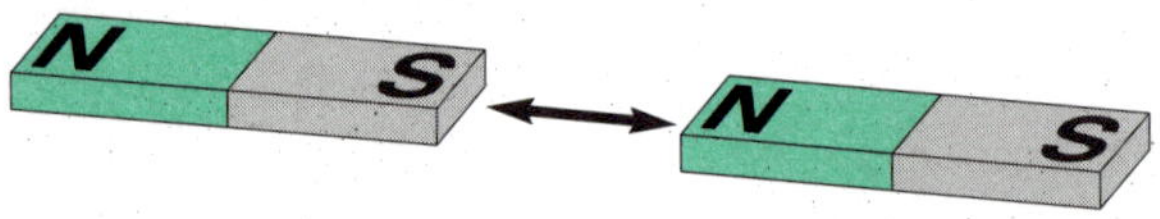

3
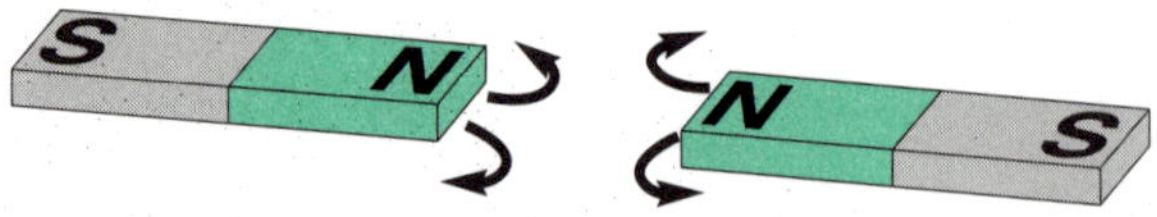

4 a) Answers will vary but should involve a magnet attracting a magnet object with a distance between them.
   b) Answers will vary but should include a magnet attracting magnetic materials through a block of wood.

Page 48

1 Paper clips next to 4 × 3 and 12 are connected by a wire on the back of the board. When she touches the wire on these paper clips the bulb lights because the circuit is complete.
2 Tick circuits B and D.

Page 49

1 Tick NO 2 Tick NO
3 a) Tick circuit C.
   b) Because there is a complete circuit

Page 50

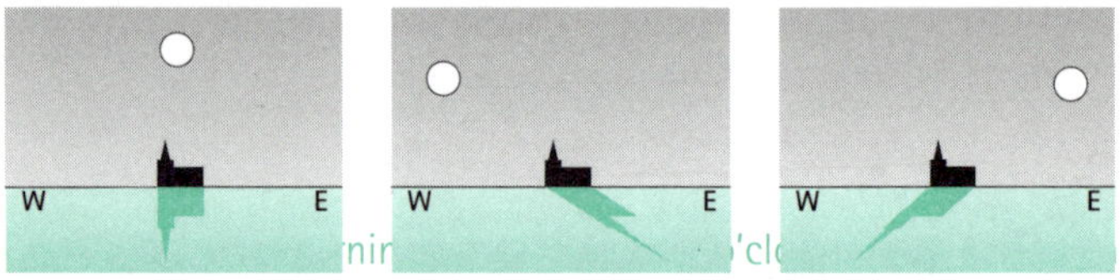

1 8 o'clock in the morning = Far right diagram
   Noon = far left diagram.
   4 o'clock in the afternoon = Central diagram
2 a) From left to right: new, crescent, half, full, gibbous
   b) Fay is right.

Page 51

1 The small parachute because there is less air resistance.
2 Arrows pointing upwards into each parachute. The arrow in the large parachute could be drawn bigger to show there is a bigger force acting on it.
3 The larger the card, the less the car travels.
4 When the card is larger there is more air resistance acting on the car.

Page 52

1 Tick: rubber. 2 Tick: pencil sharpener.
3 Tick: this will increase the friction.
4 a) Friction force. b) Newtons.

Pages 53–54

1 a) The caretaker turned on the light to check the classroom.
   b) Tick 7 o'clock.
2 a) The light fell when the TV programme was on. b) Because the teacher closed the curtains or switched off the lights.
3 a) Bright Lights let through the most light.
   b) Dimmers let through the least light.
4 Answers will vary, e.g. cover the sensor with different materials to see which lets through most light.
5 Answers will vary, e.g. how quickly sound travels.

Page 55

1 Tick: rock air and water.
2 a) The handrail.
   b) Solids c) Because Sarah could hear the sound through the handrail better.
3 Sound enters the first can making it vibrate. The vibration travels along the string to the other can. The sound can then be heard.

Page 56

1 a)
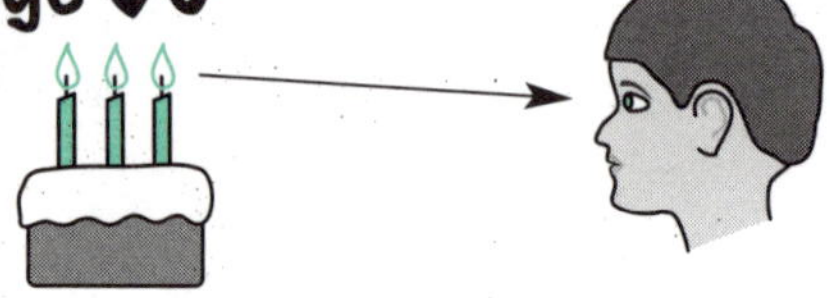

   b) Tick: The shadow is made where the light is blocked.
2 Tick: It gets smaller.
3 a) Javed measured the distance of the torch from the toy.
   b) He kept the toy in the same place.